What people are saying about

BROKEN ESCALATORS

. . .

"Great mix of comedy meets conviction. Peter's playful yet profound approach to life will definitely make you think hard and laugh often."
—*Mark Batterson, lead pastor, National Community Church, Washington D.C.; New York Times bestselling author of* The Circle Maker

"The path to promotion is never what we imagined it would be. Peter Haas brilliantly and hilariously walks us through the misconceptions of 'making it,' 'getting there,' and 'arriving.' *Broken Escalators* is part comedy, part social psychology, and part leadership training—all substantially supported with Scripture. It's not only an important read for anyone looking to grow in their spiritual, personal and professional life—it's also one of the most fun and thought-provoking books you'll pick up all year."
—*Robert Barriger, lead pastor, Camino de Vida, Lima Peru, author of* Honor Found

"In *Broken Escalators*, Peter Haas combines two of my favorite topics: Scripture and research! Utilizing his gift for comedic storytelling, Peter draws you in and makes you laugh, then pulls a one-two punch with jaw-dropping statistics and powerful myth-debunking Scripture passages. This book is light enough to make you chuckle and deep enough to make you think."

—*Rob Hoskins, President of OneHope*

"*Broken Escalators* is a funny mix of psychological studies intertwined with serious theology that makes for an interesting read. I think this book will cause readers to look deeper into their relationships with God and how their lives affect others around them."

—*Randy Bezet, lead pastor, Bayside Community Church, Bradenton, Florida*

"Now this is what the next generation of book-writing is all about! Peter Haas absolutely knows how to blend data, humor, and truth perfectly to create a fast, insightful, and hard-hitting book. His myths are on point. His research is spot on. And his truths will change you. This is a message Peter Haas was born to deliver."

—*Matt Keller, founder and lead pastor, Next Level Church in Fort Myers, Florida; author of* The Key to Everything

"Peter has always delivered the truth of God with the perfect blend of relatable comedy and sobering reality. This talent comes to life in his new book *Broken Escalators*! Let me be clear: this book is for anyone. Learn how to make better decisions, laugh more, think harder, and advance more quickly. When you're done, I'm confident you'll see God's calling on your life more clearly than ever before."

—*Rob Ketterling, lead pastor, River Valley Church, Minneapolis, Minnesota; author,* Thrill Sequence *and* Change Before You Have To

"*Broken Escalators* is a hilarious and thoughtful book jam-packed with wisdom to help anyone who feels discouraged or overlooked in their current situation. Peter is a phenomenal storyteller who uses his mishaps and missteps to open our hearts and minds so that we can learn to live happier, more fulfilled lives. He not only shares solid biblical principles, but he backs them up with scientific research you can't ignore. You'll love every minute of this great new book!"

—*John Siebeling, lead pastor, The Life Church, Memphis, Tennessee; author of* Worry-Free Finances

"Peter Haas has a sense of humor that always seems to be in high gear. He's also really smart and loves to research things nobody else cares about and comes away with a truth that we all care about. That combination makes him a great writer. If you've read *Pharisectomy*, you know what I mean. In *Broken Escalators*, Peter does it again—revealing the truth about some of the silly things we subconsciously believe. We either trust God to guide our lives or we don't. And too often we don't. This book will bring a lot of light into your life, and it'll make you laugh a lot along the way."

—*Dino Rizzo, executive director of ARC*

"*Broken Escalators* will make you laugh, and we all need to laugh more. Great mix of comedy and in-your-face truth."

—*Craig Altman, senior pastor, Grace Family Church, Temple Terrace, Florida*

"Peter fills each chapter with miracle stories that will make you laugh, challenge your mind, and cause you to rethink what it means to live promotably. This book will take you on a journey that will transform the way you live."

—*Joe Champion, founder and lead pastor, Celebration Church, Austin, Texas*

"*Broken Escalators* is seriously funny storytelling mixed with deep biblical insights. It will forever change how you make decisions about jobs, friendships, and church."

—*Herbert Cooper, senior pastor, People's Church, Oklahoma City, Oklahoma; author of* But God Changes Everything

"*Broken Escalators* is a must-read for all believers in order to gain a greater understanding of God's sovereignty. Peter takes a humorously thorough look at the many reasons God loves us enough to say no to some of our prayers. Peter also levels some of the myths of promotion and true happiness we esteem in our culture and challenges us to live a life worthy of the calling we are given. This book will turn your worldview upside down and inspire you to live the dreams God has waiting for you!"

—*Todd Mullins, lead pastor, Christ Fellowship Church, Palm Beach, Florida*

"Peter Haas is one of the most talented, spirited, and encouraging people I know! On top of that, he's written an incredible book that clearly reflects his personality—including hilarious, shocking, and true stories that may gross you out (those moths). *Broken Escalators* is relevant for anyone who has ever had a dream but has wondered why God hasn't yet busted the door wide open for them. Wait. I think that's everyone. So, I recommend this book for you, because you probably have something you need to face. My friend, Peter, covers a lot of ground to help you get past that, while saving you time and embarrassment—if you're teachable."

—*Rick Bezet, lead pastor, New Life Church, Conway, Arkansas; author of* Be Real

"I've had the privilege of knowing Peter for several years, serving together and training leaders. Peter has a unique way of blending humor and truth that makes you want to keep reading. He fills each chapter of *Broken Escalators* with miracle stories that will encourage your heart, challenge your mind, and cause you to rethink what it means to live promotably."
—*Matt Fry, lead pastor, C3 Church, Clayton, North Carolina*

"We each have our own equation of what can be summed up to create happiness. It could involve having the right job, a nice house, the perfect guy/girl, and lots of money. You might have pursued these things and found you came up short. Peter Haas has written an eye-opening book that shows a different way to true happiness and personal promotion. *Broken Escalators* is a hilarious and fascinating read—pick up this book today!"
—*Stovall Weems, founder and lead pastor, Celebration Church, Jacksonville, Florida*

"Peter's mix of humor, psychology, statistics, and theology is the perfect vehicle for exploring the concepts of promotion and happiness. This is a must-read for anyone pursuing or in a leadership role who is struggling to figure out how to keep moving up to the next level."
—*Justin Lathrop, director of strategic relationship, Assemblies of God National Resource and Leadership Center*

"Great mix of comedy, research, and deep biblical insights. *Broken Escalators* is a strategic book for anyone who wants to understand God's timing for their life. Peter's 'spoonful of sugar' approach will make people think hard and laugh often while finding the answers to life's perplexing questions."
—*Greg Surratt, founder and lead pastor, Seacoast Church, Charleston, South Carolina, and president of ARC; author of* Ir-rev-rend

BROKEN ESCALATORS

Funny & Frightful Lessons on Moth Eating and Getting to the Next Level

PETER HAAS

SALUBRIS
R E S O U R C E S

Published by Salubris Resources
1445 N. Boonville Ave.
Springfield, Missouri 65802
www.salubrisresources.com

Cover design by PlainJoe Studios (www.plainjoestudios.com)
Interior formatting by Prodigy Pixel (www.prodigypixel.com)

ISBN: 978-1-68067-021-9

18 17 16 15 ● 1 2 3 4
Printed in the United States of America

I DEDICATE THIS BOOK TO ALL THE PEOPLE WHO HAVE LISTENED TO ME WEEP THE QUESTION, "HOW LONG MUST I WAIT?" —ESPECIALLY TO MY WIFE, CAROLYN,WHO'S LOGGED THOUSANDS OF HOURS LISTENING TO ME DREAM AND PINE,AND YET SOMEHOW MANAGES BOTH TO ENCOURAGE ME AND STAY MARRIED TO ME.

CONTENTS

FOREWORD

You find them in some of the most unique places doing the most extraordinary things: people who "march to the beat of a different drummer." They are individuals who resist the undertow of status quo and, instead, radically embrace God's special purpose for their lives. These movers and dreamers make you reconsider what you think you know and inspire you to listen to your own divinely-hardwired, instinctive rhythm.

They are people like my friend Peter Haas.

Peter is one of those guys with a contagious passion for life, someone I simply love being around. He's so genuinely positive that I always feel lighter after talking with him or hearing him speak. In fact, he brings light wherever he goes—both illuminating everything and everyone around him while also lessening the weight we often feel from life's burdens. And Peter is so on-the-fly funny that I've quit eating meals with him because I inevitably end up spitting up iced tea from laughing so hard. But he also challenges me to see the truth of God's Word in dynamic new ways. He is truly a breath of fresh air.

When I heard that Peter had written a book, *Broken Escalators,* exploring both the scientific and biblical basis for true happiness, I got excited. It's a popular topic, one we all want to experience for ourselves, and I knew that in Peter's hands I would discover new truths, while laughing a lot along the way. This happy experience is the opportunity you now have before you.

Broken Escalators confirms and explains what I've come to understand about happiness from my own experiences and observations. True joyful fulfillment in life is internal—not external—and because we are spirit beings, made in God's image, we will never truly be happy until our souls prosper. This explains why superficial things never satisfy us and why some of the happiest people I know have endured hard circumstances but remain joyful because they have peace in their souls.

Few books deliver on their promise to improve your life. Too often, there's a lot of hype and spin and too little relevant substance and practical application. But that's not the case here. If you take Peter's message to heart, and laugh as hard as I know you're about to laugh, then I guarantee you'll be a happier person after reading *Broken Escalators*!

—Chris Hodges, senior pastor, Church of the Highlands, Birmingham, Alabama, and author of *Fresh Air and Four Cups*

PANTING UP ESCALATORS

When Getting to the Next Level Seems Harder Than It Should

When escalators break, it almost seems like people break with them. We stare at them with bewildered eyes—mad at the world. *How could this happen to me? Do I seriously have to use my muscles?* We don't actually say this, or our friends would start mocking us. But they're secretly lazy too.

The down-escalator, of course, always seems to be working just fine. People descend past us smugly thinking, *Suckuhs!* They don't say what they're thinking, either. And thankfully, you don't actually say your naughty response back to them. (You know what you were thinking.)

When they rope off your only route up, there's always that brief moment when you consider sprinting up the down-escalator. After all, you're (mildly) in shape. But, as you imagine your dramatic finish towards the top, suddenly, a large man, the width of the whole escalator, begins his descent. Could you handle aborting near the top? The whole mall would be watching by that point. It would be like losing at the Olympics.

My lawyer friends tell me a lot of people die on escalators (which brings a whole new meaning to the song, "Stairway to Heaven"). Escalators are notorious for sucking up loose articles of clothing.

Statistically, a huge number of people lose their pants on escalators every single day! (And for my British readers with wide eyes: I'm not referring to undergarments, lest you develop a deep, irrational fear of escalators.) Even still: How disturbing would that be? One moment you're gliding upwards in your best supermodel stance; the next, you're pantless and alone for all the world to see.

When I first heard these dark tales of pants-snatching I thought: *That's a fantastic metaphor for life. Getting to the next level in life isn't always pain-free and "pantiful."* (I made up that word. It means "to be full of pants" as in "that was a pantiful harvest.") Escalators are supposed to make our lives simpler. Yet the simplest path to our dreams isn't always the best.

We all imagine our dreams to be waiting for us on the next level. We assume that job promotions and rare opportunities will make our lives simpler and happier. We assume we know the ideal timeline for how these dreams should unfold. And we expect our parents, colleagues, spouses, and bosses—even God—to get in sync with these plans. When they don't, we throw month-long pity-parades, dedicating floats to all the people we feel have betrayed us.

You get the point. This isn't a book on the misery of escalator pants-snatching; it's a book about happiness, promotion, and all the false things we believe about our dreams. You don't realize it yet, but your brain has numerous short circuits that cause you to believe $1 + 1 = 3$ in regards to your happiness. So, more specifically, this is a book about how to avoid making dumb decisions. It's a book about why God *intentionally* breaks the "escalators" in our lives—why He slows our promotions and, out of love, *doesn't* answer our prayers in the ways we expect.

Quite frankly, some of us have a ridiculous theology of pain and promotion. We still hold fast to devastating misconceptions: that happiness is circumstantial, that people can prevent God's promotion, and, the worst misconception of all, that we know what makes us happy.

Throughout this book, we'll explore lots of research and Scriptures to prove that the very thing you're praying for could be the worst tragedy of your life. Out of this fascinating research, we'll discover ten myths of promotion and happiness that will have a dramatic effect on your ability to achieve your dreams.

STUCK ON THE DOCK

Two of my greatest joys in life wouldn't exist were it not for a magnificent mishap. The first is my church; the second is my wife.

I pastor a multisite church called Substance, based in Minneapolis. It's a fun, artsy, youth-oriented church filled with newly saved people. According to our recent survey, about 41 percent of the thousands who attend on weekends didn't attend a church or have a relationship with God even two years ago, and most of these people are under thirty years old.

The other joy in my life is Carolyn. My wife is a strong, beautiful, godly woman. And once you meet her, you'll immediately think: *Yeah, she could plant an awesome church*. But the only reason I get to experience either of these two joys is because of a misfortune that occurred in her family history.

My wife's great grandparents had tickets to sail on one of the most famous ships in history: the *Titanic*. But they showed up late and literally missed the boat! Traveling across the ocean in the early 1900s was neither simple nor cheap. So even though it makes a great story now, at the time, missing their chance to get on the *Titanic* was devastating. I guarantee you, there were tears falling while they sat on that dock and watched their dreamboat float away. If they were feisty like my wife and I, they probably had a good fight: "Why didn't you just stop and ask for directions back there?" "I told you we needed to get here earlier."

Carolyn's great grandmother probably pictured herself at the bow of the ship, leaning into the wind with arms stretched wide, hair streaming in the breeze, Celine Dion singing in the background. But instead, they were stuck on a stupid dock, with all of their junk piled around them, waiting and wondering why this had happened.

In those days, it took a while before they discovered the *Titanic* had sunk. In fact, they didn't know until they subsequently found themselves on one of the boats that picked up survivors.

Looking back, it's easy to say, "Wow! I'm glad they missed that ship!" The ramifications are staggering:

- My wife wouldn't have been born
- The church my wife helped to plant wouldn't exist
- My three delightful kids wouldn't be alive today
- I don't know if I would have even found faith in God were it not for my wife

So, *now*, it's easy to see how God used a devastating moment to bless a lot of people, but at the time, none of these future blessings were clear.

Thus, the stunning paradox is this: *Your current devastation may be the greatest thing that has happened to you.* Your current delay just might be your current deliverance. As you'll see throughout this book, God loves to overcome evil and pain in two ways: He removes it, or He ingeniously thwarts it (see John 16:33). Yes, we often prefer the first choice, but what a poetic culmination it is when He turns our pain into a platform, our tests into testimonies.

As a result, I lovingly remind you: The timeline we have for our lives is often totally out of sync with God's, because we can't see what He sees and we don't know what He knows. So when our lives don't look a certain way within a certain schedule, we're devastated. We're weeping on the dock, not realizing that our dreams were *Titanic* nightmares. They were a slow freezing death . . . a pantless promotion—an inglorious, tedious stairway to death.

When life gets tough, when dreamboats float away, I've watched many good people become senseless. They dive into the water and frantically swim towards their departing *Titanic* shouting, "This is my last chance to reach my dreams! Besides, it's the newest and best ship! It's unsinkable!" Or back to our escalator analogy, they feel like "everyone is gliding up—but me!"

Sometimes it feels like everyone's dreams are coming true except yours. Your idiot friend lands a dream job and spouse. Fertile Myrtle gets pregnant, *again*. And there we are, panting our way up the broken escalator, knowing that it shouldn't feel this difficult and desperately hoping God will jerk our stairway back into motion.

Might I suggest there's more at play here? Perhaps God is concerned with something far greater than building your dreams. Perhaps His dream is to build *you*.

MIXED MESSAGES

Recently Carolyn was surfing one of her favorite social networking sites and found a picture of a friend who also happened to be one of our church members. My wife typed: "Girl, you look stinkin' hot after that baby!" But after pressing return, my face suddenly popped up next to this comment. It turns out that Carolyn was accidentally logged into *my* account! It was a horrifying moment. To make matters worse, Carolyn couldn't figure out how to delete her remark, so she frantically called me for tech support—a phone call that didn't exactly go smoothly.

Now, keep in mind, I'm a pastor who has a lot of people following me online. And although people love having an encouraging pastor, there are simply some things you *don't* want your pastor to tell you. One of those is: "Girl, you look stinkin' hot after that baby!"

Generally speaking, my wife and I speak to one another in peaceful tones, but when I was suddenly thrust into a tech support role with my entire reputation on the line, I was anything but peaceful. I suddenly understood how Carolyn's ancestors felt when their ship was floating away—or, in my case, my reputation. With every passing second, my name was changing from Pastor Peter to Predatory Pete. To make matters worse, Carolyn's updated software had conveniently changed all of the known "delete post" functions.

After a few shouts and apologies, we managed to "slay" Predatory Pete. To this day, I don't know how many people saw that post, but whenever I see that particular woman at church, I go out of my way to speak very formally to her—and to compliment her husband every chance I get. Carolyn and I learned a valuable lesson through our social media trauma: We don't always know what we're doing, and we can't always control what's happening. Sometimes we feel stuck on a broken escalator, and we need help. So consider this book your escalator repair guide.

Throughout the book we're going to look at fascinating questions like:

- What are the scientific causes of anxiety?
- What are the statistical predictors of happiness?
- Why does it feel like some people experience "promotion" more easily than others?
- What are the little known "myths of promotion" that regularly sucker people into bad jobs, moves, and relationships?
- How do we pursue our callings without falling prey to these myths?

Some of these research-driven myths will be obvious. Others will be counterintuitive. Through all of the questions, however, my goal is to show that perhaps everything we believe about happiness and everything we're praying for is wrong—or, at the very least, missing the greater point.

As you read this book, there's a good chance you're waiting on something: a dream spouse, a dream job, a family, or a golden opportunity. Perhaps you're waiting for healing—physical, marital, or financial. Seasons of waiting can be excruciating. But by the time you're done with this book, you just might thank God for the delays. In fact, one of the greatest confirmations of God's love is that He *doesn't* answer most of our prayers. If that sounds strange, then you, my friend, should get ready for the ride of your life. It's a lot like the time I took my three kids to a theme park.

Theme parks are a rite of passage for parents. Both the trauma and joy of taking your family to one will change a person. When our kids were younger, we'd wait in line, but every time we'd get to the front, one of my daughters would suddenly refuse to get on! So we'd have to step out of line to have the "you're not going to die (unless you keep doing this to me) speech." I will never force them to go on a ride they don't want to, but usually, in these situations, *they* were the ones begging to go on the ride, and then they'd freak out about that very same ride.

Finally, on one such trip, I was exhausted. We were at the tail end of a mile-long line, and suddenly it happened: "Daddy, I don't wanna go!" Although I'm ashamed to admit it, I just lost it. I started speaking in my "monster voice." You know, the voice you use to say something like: "I brought you kids into this world, and I can take you out, too!"

On that day, my monster blurted out: "Would you just shut up, and enjoy the ride!" Carolyn faked a smile at me while her eyes shouted, "Peter, you're losing your mind!"

There's nothing quite like shouting at people to get them to enjoy things. I realize it's an unconventional strategy. I can't argue that it's biblical. However, when used sparingly, a well-crafted, bloodthirsty threat can sometimes jumpstart a whole lot of fun. And sure enough, at the end of the ride, all my kids, including the one who had dissented, shouted, "Again, Daddy! Let's do it again!"

In a similar fashion, I believe our loving heavenly Father would say to many of us, "Would you shut up and enjoy the ride?" The Hebrew version of this is probably more accurately translated: "Be still and know that I am God" (Ps. 46:10).

God knows, there are only two ways to experience the rollercoaster of life: You can throw your hands up and enjoy it, or you can try to control it. (Good luck with that second option, by the way.)

"But I'll barf," you complain.

Then I say, "Find a friend who can make you laugh between barfs." There's nothing funnier (well, maybe a few things) than a *barf-laugh* (pronounced, *bar-FLAF*—I made that word up; make sure you accent the second syllable). Life is simply too short to spend hemming and hawing, complaining or pining.

Like my wife's great grandparents, you won't always understand why your dream ship leaves without you. But that's the point. We don't really know *anything*, which is why we need these two things:

1. A Father in heaven who can look out for us.
2. An unflinching trust in His plan, no matter how things look.

Bottom line, let's pray more for promotability and less for promotion. Let's work more on having the type of heart God can bless and less on doctoring the circumstances that will bless our hearts. Let's enjoy the rollercoaster of life, like a ride to be enjoyed, more than a trauma to be controlled. And in accepting these ideas, our escalators will once again become a fun carnival ride (which is ironically how escalators began) and not merely a means to an end.

With all this in mind, I'm excited to introduce you to the art, science, and Scriptures behind promotion and happiness.

WHO'S YOUR DADDY?

The Strange Science of Anxiety and How Various Religions Deal With It

'll never forget the first time I prayed in public. I was a fresh believer in a charismatic church, and everyone else at the prayer meeting seemed like a prayer-ninja. They would flip and kick through the prayer list with the most fluid and poetic prayers I had ever heard, quoting Scriptures and Hebrew names of God I had never heard before. Then, the worst of all things happened. One of the leaders asked me to pray.

"Me? Out loud?" I asked in horror. It was like being asked to free-style dance after a professional just flipped off the stage. I'm pretty sure I prayed like a caveman, "God . . . uh, me no pray good."

So in that first month, I picked up a few tricks to spice up my prayer-ninja-dance routine and discovered that people are certain to be impressed by your super-spiritual sounding prayers if you do the following:

1. **SHOUT AND CAST SOMETHING OUT WHEN YOU PRAY.**

   If little Emily needs you to pray for her boo-boo, your job is to yell the Devil out of her . . . just in case.

2. USE LOTS OF FIRE METAPHORS.

("Consume us with your flaming smoke of fire!") Alternate these with water analogies. ("Flood us with your dripping river of rain, O God.") And follow the general rule: Shout during the fire; whisper during the rain. When you run out of words, simply exhale loudly as if you're giving birth. (No offense to those of you who have actually delivered a baby.).

3. QUOTE AN OBSCURE BIBLE VERSE.

It doesn't even have to make sense. A weird verse from Leviticus about cloven hooves and oxen will do fine. Just quote it passionately and talk your way into a metaphor about the marriage supper of the Lamb. When other people in the room hear this, their confusion will quickly morph into a deep respect over your spiritual insight—assuming you make this transition confidently. Act like everyone should know what you're talking about.

4. SALT YOUR PRAYERS WITH OBSCURE NAMES OF GOD.

My favorite deep-in-the-Spirit-sounding names are Jehovah Tsidkenu or Mekaddishkem. (Make sure you hack out the gutteral sounds like a native Hebrew speaker.) You also might try quoting Amy Grant's song "El Shaddai" in the middle of your prayer as if you're spontaneously making it up. (Be careful. Many young people these days don't know the song and may be so impressed that they'll want you to mentor them after doing this; then your pretentious jig is truly history.)

5. ADD A COOL ACCENT.

American's love it when British or Australian people pray. After trying it for a month, though, I was harshly told that "you actually have to be from there in order to do it." So use this technique sparingly, like when you're visiting a new church.

Bear in mind that I'm not saying God actually likes these techniques. If you want God to actually hear your prayers, you may want to apply different advice.

But seriously . . . our prayers do reveal a lot about our theology. Jesus pointed out that, if our prayer lives are dominated with anxiety and asking God for things, then we probably don't have an authentic relationship with God the Father.

Don't misunderstand me. It's okay to "ask God for things." Jesus repeatedly encouraged this (Matt. 7:7; John 15:7). However, God "knows what we need even before we ask" (Matt. 6:8), so if we spend an inordinate amount of time asking Him for things, it's a symptom of a greater disease: *spiritual Fatherlessness*. Allow me to explain.

It's interesting to note that, of all the names of God that Jesus used when He prayed, He used the name Father the most. Why? The answer to this question can revolutionize your relationship with God. By the end of this chapter, we'll discover that, relating to God as Father can literally alter your brain's chemistry and reduce your odds of being anxious. I realize that sounds like a sensational claim. But after a bizarre mix of stories on drugs, chopping up brains, and other fun facts, I'm going to show you why Christianity has a scientifically different effect on our bodies compared to other religions. By the end, you'll be able to answer the question: Am I even experiencing these benefits?

WHO'S YOUR DADDY?

Although praying to "the Father" may sound routine to modern believers, to first-century Jews, it was an astounding novelty. According to scholars, Jews have never commonly referred to God as "Father."[1] And yet, Old Testament prophecies hinted that when the Messiah came, His Father would be of a divine origin.[2] Jesus stated that His purpose was to "reveal the Father" (Matt. 11:27). He constantly implored people to go beyond knowing God as "Lord" and instead call Him "Father" (Matt. 7:21). Jesus, for instance, emphasized the Father's desire to be generous: "If you, then, though you are evil, know how to give good gifts to your children, how much more will your Father in heaven give good gifts to those who ask him!" (Matt. 7:11). That's why, in John 17:6, Jesus prayed "Father, I have manifested your name to the men you gave me." To be clear: who's name did Jesus manifest? *The Father's.*

The idea of fatherhood has somewhat lost its meaning in our culture. For the past fifty years or so, fathers have too often been stereotyped as clueless breadwinners. One in three Americans now grow up in single-parent homes—most of them with only a mother. And remember that until the 1700s, people generally didn't commute to work. Most kids were apprenticed into Dad's trade—separation from Dad and segmentation of children by age is a relatively modern idea. All these things contribute to a concept of fatherhood that's far weaker than the way most people in other periods of history would have understood it.

QUITE SIMPLY, IF YOU TRULY KNOW GOD AS YOUR FATHER, YOU'LL LIVE COMPLETELY DIFFERENTLY, AND THIS WILL RID YOU OF SPIRITUAL ANXIETY AS WELL.

There's been a huge amount of research on the power fathers have on child-outcomes, and if you make a list of fifty negative behaviors—from drug abuse to domestic violence, from suicide to sexual confusion—almost every one of them skyrockets where there has been an absentee father. Studies have even found a direct correlation between chronic anxiety and fatherlessness.[3] So it's not a stretch to believe that spiritual fatherlessness has a profound effect on anxiety too. Quite simply, if you truly know God as your Father, you'll live completely differently, and this will rid you of spiritual anxiety as well.

LEARNING FATHERHOOD FROM A DAUGHTER

My wife lost her father to suicide just before her seventeenth birthday. She lived through a devastating tragedy. Yet, she learned early on to trust God to be a "father to the fatherless" (Ps. 68:5), and she has never been afraid to ask her heavenly Father for practical things. This ability has always been inspiring to me.

For example, one time she noticed that our two young girls were completely outgrowing their clothes, so in her prayer journal, she wrote: "Father, you see that our girls need more clothes. And you see that we don't have the money. I trust you to completely take care of our girls." Then she wrote the exact date and time next to this entry. A few days later, we got a gift card in the mail. A farmer in the area had been praying, and with the card, he wrote a note: "I just sensed that God wanted to bless your daughters today; so I bought you a gift card." Of course, it happened to be a gift card for a super-hip clothing store. (And it's a miracle that a farmer in central Wisconsin even knew about this store.) But, get this—the receipt showed that he bought the gift card online at the *exact same moment* my wife journaled her prayer. Is that a coincidence?

Later that month our lawn mower died, and I was totally irritated. After all, there were a million other things I wanted to spend money on—and we didn't have money for more than one or two of them. That same day, Carolyn and I had to go to a wedding, so as we jumped in the car, I started whining about our lawn mower. Immediately, Carolyn responded, "Well, let's trust God for one."

When she said that I have to admit I was a little annoyed. Here I was having a great moan session about my lawn equipment, and she went hyper-spiritual on me. I almost said back, "That's ridiculous!" But a small part of my heart agreed, and I thought, *Well, why not? What have we got to lose?* As we drove off to the wedding, Carolyn prayed, "Father, you see that we need a lawn mower. You've been faithful in the past, and You'll be faithful in the future. Amen."

In light of earlier prayer guidelines, you'll agree that my wife's prayer wasn't very impressive. No shouting. No demon-casting. No obscure Bible promises or strange names. Her prayer was short, simple, and full of thanksgiving.

When we came home from the wedding three hours later, there was a new lawn mower sitting in front of our garage! I looked at my wife thinking, *Did you call someone or borrow someone's lawn mower just to impress me? But she looked as surprised as I did.*

"I didn't tell anyone anything!" she promised.

A note taped to the handle explained:

Dear pastor,

My mom sold her house. She had this brand new lawn mower and needs to get rid of it. I figured that you'll know someone in our church who could use this! Call me if you don't, and I'll pick it up.

Carolyn smiled at me and said simply, "God is good."

In that moment, I remember thinking, *I truly don't know God like she does.* At least, I didn't trust Him like she did. Despite all my theological training, I didn't have a heavenly "Dad." But from that point on, I made it my goal to start talking to God about practical things.

The same month as my lawn mower lesson, our church built a half-

> JESUS SAID WE DON'T NEED TO PRAY LENGTHY OR HYPER-SPIRITUAL PRAYERS—HE ALREADY KNOWS WHAT WE NEED.

pipe skate ramp for our youth ministry. I grew up riding freestyle BMX on a big half-pipe ramp in my backyard, so I was excited to finish our church ramp. Whenever the skaters came over, I'd usually skate with them instead of bike. The only problem was, I needed a new skateboard deck. So I thought, *Here's my opportunity: God, I could use a new skateboard.* And, no exaggeration, later that very day, one of the new guys in our youth ministry asked me, "Pastor, would you have any use for an extra skateboard? I just got a brand new deck." In the weeks that followed, it felt like every time I asked God for a favor, He supernaturally provided.

While this was happening, I couldn't help but think what Jesus said in Matthew 6:8, "Your Father knows what you need before you ask him." And later in chapter 6, verse 31 continues, "Do not worry, saying, 'What shall we eat?' or 'What shall we drink?' or 'What shall we wear?' For the pagans run after all these things, and your heavenly Father knows that you need them." In the same sermon, Jesus also said, "If you, then, though you are evil, know how to give good gifts to your children, how much more will your Father in heaven give good gifts to those who ask him!" (Matt. 7:11).

In other words, you don't have to worry about stuff! You don't merely have a God—you have a Father! Jesus said we don't need to pray lengthy or hyper-spiritual prayers—He already knows what we need. Indeed, we don't even need to waste much time asking for things. Instead, Jesus argued, spend your time *"hallowing His name."* And what name is that? "Our *Father* in heaven."

WE'RE IN CHARGE HERE!

In the book *Stumbling on Happiness* (which inspired numerous chapters of this book), Harvard psychologist Daniel Gilbert says "the human being is the only animal that truly thinks about the future."[4] He continues, "The greatest achievement of the human brain is its ability to imagine objects and episodes that do not exist in the realm of the real."[5]

Now, it's true that most mammals instinctively anticipate the future, but none of them have the capacity to strategically analyze it. By contrast, when humans imagine themselves living in outer space, we figure out a way to do it—even if it requires us to create a hundred new technologies to make it work. Creative strategizing is one of the attributes that sets us apart from everything else God has made.

When the Bible says that we are distinctly made in the "image and likeness of God," it raises the question *how*? After pondering a little more science and Scripture, I'd like to make a few suggestions I think you'll find intriguing.

When Adam and Eve were placed in the garden of Eden, their job was to "rule and subdue" creation. God gave human beings the power of *creative governance*. Their job was to name animals, to organize and maintain the things the Creator made. We almost get the sense that God was planning on creating millions of more planets just like ours. He told them to "be fruitful and multiply," so He would have an ever-expanding team of helpers to assist in governing His endless creation projects. But the main point is this: Unlike any other animal, we can use our imaginations to see into the future. We can conceive things that don't exist and then create them. We are like God in that we are creative about the future.

The Bible seems to imply that before sin entered the world our creative powers were effortless. But after sin, Genesis 3:17–19 says that from now on, "cursed is the ground because of you; through painful toil you will eat food from it all the days of your life. . . . By the sweat of your brow you will eat your food."

The text implies that up until this point, tending the garden had never required sweat; it was never painful. There was never any *toil*. However, that observation brings up the question: How, then, did they tend the garden without toilsome work?

Some believe God originally designed people to "work through speaking"—much the way God created the world. He spoke, "Let there be light," and there was light (Gen. 1:3).

Since we were created in the image and likeness of God, some people think two of the attributes that make us "like God" compared to all other animals are:

1. WE HAVE AN UNPARALLELED ABILITY TO THINK CREATIVELY ABOUT THE FUTURE.
2. JUST LIKE GOD, OUR WORDS HAVE CREATIVE POWER.

So it appears that, when Adam and Eve sinned, God essentially said, "I'm going to take some of this power away. From now on, you'll have to work for what you need. Or, at the very least, you'll have to restore your faith in Me." Interestingly, Jesus also said, "By your words you will be acquitted, and by your words you will be condemned" (Matt. 12:27). There are many Bible accounts where God was particularly harsh on believers who used their words poorly (see Num. 11:1–3; Luke 1:18–20; 1:59–64).

Thankfully, however, we can reclaim portions of this remarkable power. Jesus said, "If you have faith and don't doubt," you can curse this fig tree or tell that mountain to move (Matt. 21:21). Or as Paul put it, we can produce work through faith rather than sweat (1 Thess.1:3).

After God started providing me with gift cards, lawn mowers, and skateboards, I started to wonder if my prayers and intimacy with the Father were more important than I had previously understood.

But how does relating to God as a Father alter your brain's chemistry—not to mention your anxiety? After a horrifying history lesson, we're going to learn about a part of your brain called the "prefrontal cortex." And once you understand what that part of your brain does, it may change the way you interpret some of Christ's most famous words.

CHOPPING UP BRAINS AND THE SCIENCE OF ANXIETY

Over the last few decades, scientists have discovered that the part of the brain responsible for "thinking ahead" is called the prefrontal cortex.[6] And unfortunately, doctors figured this out the hard way.

Back in 1940s and '50s, there was a popular surgery called a lobotomy, in which doctors would strategically sever that part of the brain in people who suffered with extreme anxiety. After severing the connection in the brain with a surgical knife, these people would become super-relaxed. (Some of you are thinking, *Sign me up!* But hold that thought.)

Ironically, the medical experts didn't foresee a significant side effect of the operation. Once surgeons disconnected this part of the brain, none of the same patients could plan for the future. Sure, they worried less, but, if you asked them, "What do you want to do tomorrow?" they would go blank. It's like someone telling someone to think about infinity. Human beings simply don't have the capacity to imagine the infinite. In the same

TO IMAGINE THE FUTURE WITHOUT THE COMPLETE SECURITY OF OUR HEAVENLY FATHER IS TERRIFYING.

24

way, when lobotomy patients were asked to plan their vacation next week, they simply couldn't wrap their minds around it.

So the gruesome yet powerful revelation was this: Anxiety comes from the same part of the brain that helps us think about the future. When we think about the future and feel out of control, it causes us to feel anxious.

In other words, the ability that makes us unique among all other creatures is the same brain function that causes us to feel anxious. Or, to frame this in a biblical context: to imagine the future without the complete security of our heavenly Father is terrifying. After sin entered the world, we lost that intimacy—which means the very organ that enabled us to dream can now also torture us.

In the introduction, I explained that I would reveal the myths about happiness or promotion. So, our first one is:

MYTH

THE ANXIETY MYTH:
If I don't worry, my dreams won't stay on track.

Although anxiety comes from thinking about the future, God the Father doesn't want us to be anxious—unless, of course, we deny Him. But before exploring Christ's unique way of dealing with anxiety, let's explore how other religions try to solve this.

TRY A LITTLE DENIAL

Those of you who've studied Hinduism (or other forms of Eastern Yoga) know that Eastern meditation obsesses over "being present in the *now*"—not the past or the future. In other words, Hindus achieve peace by *living in the present*. If we think about this from a scientific standpoint, the associated meditations are basically a clever technique for ignoring the part of our brain that's driving us nuts, the prefrontal cortex.

However, the Bible teaches a completely different way of achieving peace. I'll reduce the process down to three simple steps:

1. **GET A HEAVENLY FATHER.**

2. **USE PRAYER AND PETITION TO COMMUNICATE WITH GOD—** which reinforces both your relationship to the Father and your sense of security.

3. **GIVE THANKS WHEN PRESENTING YOUR REQUESTS TO GOD.** In doing so, the Bible promises that, "the peace of God, which transcends all understanding, will guard your hearts and your minds in Christ Jesus" (Phil. 4:6–7).

By contrast, Hinduism and Eastern Yoga reason that if your lack of control is what causes anxiety, then simply ignore your need to have control! But Jesus says, "No! Don't ignore your need to control. Rather, get a Father who can control it. Don't stop thinking about the future because, frankly, you need to think about it. Heaven and hell are real." Indeed, Jesus points out, "I want you to think about it so much that you actually 'store up treasure in heaven'" (Matt. 6:20). Yet at the same time, He argues, "Don't worry about it. You have a Father who will help you."

GOD WANTS TO RESTORE OUR CAPACITY TO DREAM!

In other words, if we have a heavenly Father, we don't need to live in denial of our future or fear of our lack of control. And in doing the three disciplines noted above, God literally redeems our prefrontal cortex—the uniquely human part of our brains.

To put this in less nerdy terms: God wants to restore our capacity to dream! He wants us to look to the future and speak things into existence with awe-inspiring confidence and creativity. We speak forth passion into our marriages, clarity to our children's callings, peace into our workplaces, joy into our friendships, and richness into every area of our lives.

CAN I DO WEED AND LOVE JESUS?

So far we've talked about how some people turn to Hinduism for peace, but other people turn to a different "religion" to solve the anxiety problem: drugs.

In our church filled with newly saved people, I'm regularly asked, "Can I get drunk or do weed and still love Jesus? After all, didn't Stephen, the disciple get 'stoned'?" (At least they've read their Bibles, kind of). Stephen was under the influence of a different kind of spirit, the Holy Spirit (Acts 7:55).

The Bible offers a spiritual alternative to drugs called the Holy Spirit (Eph. 5:18). Strangely enough, the biblical manifestations of the Holy Spirit can sometimes be confused with drunkenness or joy (Acts 2:13–15; 1 Cor. 14:23).

Not all drugs are bad. If you've been diagnosed with certain illnesses, God has inspired many marvelous medications to help with that. But drugs like marijuana have terrible side effects—especially in young people whose brains are still developing. After all, guess what part of the brain is most affected by pot? Yep. The prefrontal cortex—and the dreams it produces about the future.

Long-term marijuana use is the chemical equivalent of a lobotomy.

That's why people who regularly smoke pot lose their ability to do long-term planning. Studies show that when kids under sixteen do marijuana, they're especially susceptible to this type of brain damage.[7] That means they lose their ability to dream, to feel, to anticipate the future, and to speak creatively towards it. And not only that, it decreases the user's IQ, life-expectancy, and ability to problem-solve.[8]

Thankfully, our heavenly Father offers a better solution. The apostle Peter wrote, "The end of all things is near. Therefore be alert and of sober mind so that you may pray" (1 Peter 5:7). In other words, we don't need to ignore the future or fill our minds with haze. We can look forward to the "end of all things" as we pray. And, again, to whom should we pray? The Father.

THE BIG REVELATION

As we conclude this first leg of our ride up the escalator, let's think about Jesus on the night He was betrayed by Judas. You might think Jesus would have been a mess! (And in some ways, He probably felt like a mess before He prayed in the garden of Gethsemane.) Yet, when the betrayal actually happened, Jesus showed incredible poise. He was so connected to His heavenly Father that He was capable of whipping out a miracle that saved Peter's life (see Luke 22:50–51).

Why was Jesus at peace? Because He connected with His Father through prayer. He used the three steps I told you about earlier: (1) acknowledged His Father; (2) used prayer and petition; and (3) gave thanks. So when the crazy stuff went down—when Peter swung his sword—notice what Jesus told him: "Do you think I cannot call on my Father, and he will at once put at my disposal more than twelve legions of angels?" (Matt. 26:53).

Twelve legions is roughly equivalent to 72,000 angels, and keep in mind, it only took one angel in the Old Testament to put 185,000 men to death (2 Kings 19:35). Jesus was saying to Peter: "Do you realize how much power we have? Do you realize how much love comes from our Father? We don't need to flail around using our carnal strength! The Father and I are purposefully allowing this to happen!"

Ultimately, God wants us to live with towering levels of confidence, even in the midst of betrayal. He wants us to be optimistic about the future. Our ability to plan was meant to be bathed in *divine optimism,* even when we take up crosses. We were meant to live, dripping in the Father's love, saturated in the confidence of His faithfulness. To lack these attributes is to miss the whole point of being "born again," to be a child *again* who doesn't need to worry about anything except obedience.

This raises the question: Do you have that kind of relationship? Have you welcomed Him into your current circumstances? If you're interested, read this paraphrase of the Lord's Prayer in Matthew 6:9–13:

Father, we acknowledge, You are not some detached and impersonal God. You are our Father in heaven. We make Your name hallowed, sacred, and special—which means, we celebrate this intimate attribute in You. We ask for Your heavenly plan to manifest in our lives knowing You provide daily bread for us. We will live innocently today—free of grudges and unforgiveness in response to Your gift of forgiveness. Help us to avoid all alternative ways of living, and deliver us from traps of evil, through Your infinite power, that we will forever revel in. Amen.

KEY IDEAS

1. The way we pray is often an indicator of many things such as the myths we believe and the way we view God.

2. Of all the names Jesus used to refer to God, Father was the most common. There's a large amount of theological significance that can be attached to this.

3. When you understand what it means to have God as a Father, it alters how you live.

4. Unlike any other animal, humans can use our imaginations to see into the future, conceive things that don't exist, and then create them. We are like God in that we are creative about the future.

5. After sin entered the world, our creative powers were severely impaired, along with our intimacy and security with our Creator.

6. Scriptures indicate that our words were once an infinitely greater source of power.

7. Science shows that anxiety comes from the same part of the brain that thinks about the future.

8. Some religions, such as Hinduism, attempt to bring about peace by avoiding thoughts of the future—by living in the "now." But this bypasses the very ability that makes humans exceptional.

9. Drugs, such as marijuana, decrease anxiety but simultaneously destroy the part of our brains that thinks and dreams about the future. This, too, destroys the very gift that makes humans exceptional.

10. Rather than bypassing this part of our brains, Jesus taught us to redeem our humanity by getting a heavenly Father—which enables us to look to the future and speak things into existence with awe-inspiring creativity and confidence— free of the anxiety that comes from spiritual fatherlessness.

DISCUSSION QUESTIONS

1. If you could speak in a different cool accent, which would you pick?

2. How would you describe your relationship with your earthly father? Close, distant, nonexistent?

3. How might your relationship with your earthly father affect how you perceive the heavenly Father?

4. Do you ever pray? Have you ever experienced a miraculous answer to prayer?

5. Have you ever had a season when your prayer life was dominated by asking God for things? In light of this chapter, what do you think might change?

6. What are you most anxious about right now? If you were fully convinced your heavenly Father was taking care of you, how would it change things?

7. After learning about our creativity and the power of our words, does it change the way you think about complaining or cursing? Why or why not?

8. What are some of the ways—good and bad—that you cope with anxiety?

9. What was the most interesting factoid or takeaway out of this chapter and why?

10. If you knew God would help you achieve your dreams, what would you dare to accomplish over the next twenty years or a lifetime?

EXPLODING POTTY BUCKETS

What If Traumatic Experiences and Unanswered Prayers Are
the Best Things That Can Happen to Us?

The great American family road trip is a rite of passage. When I was a kid, my parents would take us on three-week camping trips to the Grand Canyon in a conversion van with no seatbelts. Before iPhones, car televisions, and decent portable video games, parents used to entertain kids with pure danger. Dad could slam on the brakes at any moment, and suddenly, little sister (and our Battleship game) would explode across the dashboard. It was thrilling. We never knew how many family members would make it home alive. It entertained us for hours on end.

Equally entertaining was our road trip "potty-bucket"—fashioned out of an old ice cream pail. We had it because, within ten minutes of our last potty break, someone would inevitably cry out: "I've gotta go, soooo bad!" So the potty bucket was an efficient problem-solver for Mom and Dad—and novel entertainment for the rest of us. But, like many fine traditions, it ended one time when my older sister used it on the back bench seat. With an ear-splitting crack, the shattering ice cream pail reminded us that efficiency needs boundaries.

Out of respect for my parents, I won't repeat what they said that day, but when you have kids, trust me in this, you'll say things you never expected to say. Now that I have three children of my own, I'm continually shocked by the commands that fly out of my mouth. For example, I once had to tell one of my kids, "Can you avoid sucking on your sister's hairbrush?" And another time: "We do not splash family members with toilet water!" (As these words came out of my mouth, I thought, *This is not a boundary I ever imagined having to lay down.*) Or "Hey! Do not balance that bowl of hot soup on your brother's shirtless chest!" (Kids are very creative.)

And how about this actual interchange?

Me: "Stop sitting on your sister's head!"
Daughter: "I'm not sitting. I'm jumping."

Outside of parenthood, where else would we ever get the chance to offer such meaningful guidelines for life? A few staff meetings I've chaired have come close but not quite there.

My wife once had to give this command: "We do not *lick* our armpits at the kitchen table!" To which I responded: "I'm sooo sorry baby. I'm setting a terrible example right now." In my defense, you have to understand that my kids challenged me that licking your own armpit wasn't possible, and of course, I had to show them that, as the man of the house, I could do anything. (I'll bet some of you are trying it right now while others of you are questioning the spiritual value of this book.)

So now that I'm "all grown up," I take my own monkeys on road trips. On one trip, I knew it was only a matter of time before one of these ludicrous commands would come out of my mouth. But the first one erupted even before we got out of the driveway!

As we stood beside our overloaded minivan, the family stared at

me as I cast an inspiring vision for the road trip ahead: "Yes, we're going to spend the next two days in the car. But at the end of our eight-hour drive today, we're going to hit a hotel with an epic swimming pool!"

Relying on my many years of rousing people with vision, I spoke about this legendary pool filled with mystical waters. My son, Eden—at the time a precocious three-year-old—listened, enraptured, eyes wide. Even though the pool was five hundred miles away, we could already smell its overly-chlorinated glory. Before I could finish my speech, Eden ran around the minivan to grab his thick foam swim jacket and started clicking it around his small body.

"Wait a second, Eden," I explained. "We won't get to the pool until later."

"Dad, I know! I just want to get ready for it!"

After jamming his water-winged body into his car seat, he struggled to stretch the five-point harness over his bulging life jacket. And that's when the bizarre one-liner spewed from my mouth: "Buddy, you can't wear your big, foam swim jacket on an eight-hour car ride! That's crazy!"

Eden looked at me resolutely and said with his eyes, "You wanna bet?"

Carolyn backed me up: "Eden you're going to be hot, cranky, and sweaty! You can barely fit into your car seat."

But he insisted, convinced the burdensome jacket would somehow increase his pleasure and remind him of the destination.

We relented, and as the minivan pulled out of the driveway, Eden was beaming. But twenty minutes later, the classic kid-question hit: "Daddy, are we there yet?"

I knew it was going to be a long day.

In an hour, sweat dribbled down Eden's face: "Daddy, why aren't we there yet?"

My every word of encouragement fell on deaf ears, and about four hours in, Eden started weeping, "Daddy, you *promised* there'd be a pool!" By hour six, he closed his eyes and whimpered, "Daddy, don't you love me?"

We've all been there, haven't we? We're on the journey towards a perfect job, the dream marriage, the fully functional family, and we pray, "God, are we there yet? Why isn't it happening?" We set our goals, bolstering our entitlement by quoting Scriptures at God. We command the sun to stand still (Joshua 10). We put on the bulky "swim jacket of faith" and heat up our lives with sweaty anticipation. And, to be sure, sometimes this works well for us. Sometimes these prayers actually work the way we want them to. That's what makes Christianity so confusing at times: Miracles do actually occur . . . but not always when we want them.

At our church, for example, we've seen people get supernaturally healed of cancer, burns, and blindness. A doctor who witnessed one of these miracles was so amazed that he quit his practice to become a missionary. But before you overestimate the spirituality of our church, we also have a lot of people who are not getting healed. So we are tempted to ask (loudly), "What's up with that?"

Fortunately, the Bible offers dozens of reasons for unanswered prayer. Here are a few:

1. A LACK OF INTEGRITY (James 4:3; 1 Peter 3:7) **OR FAITH** (Mark 6:5–6).

2. A LACK OF PERSISTENCE (LUKE 18:1).

3. A LACK OF PRAYING IN ACCORDANCE WITH GOD'S WILL
(1 JOHN 5:14–15).

For example, if you're praying, "God help me rob a bank this Saturday," you may have a harder time going to church on Sunday—both emotionally and physically. But what if you are praying in sync with Scripture? Healing is promised throughout the Bible, but what if it's still not happening?

4. SPIRITUAL WARFARE.

Ephesians 6 talks about angels and demons that do battle in response to people's prayers. Daniel 10:13 talks about an angel who was delayed twenty-one days because of spiritual warfare. I could probably write an entire book on these four reasons alone, but the fifth reason is perhaps the most interesting.

5. GOD IS WORKING TO BRING ABOUT AN EVEN GREATER GOOD.

Sometimes God will use difficulty to draw us into deeper intimacy with Him (2 Cor. 1:9). For some of us, trials are the only way God can grab our attention. And there's a huge theme in Scripture that suggests God is more interested in the character and faith of His people than in quick miracles or a life without trials. God loves to turn tests into testimonies, pains into platforms, mangers into magnificence.

When God gave the Israelites the Promised Land, for instance, there's a rather strange Scripture in Judges 3:1: "These are the nations the LORD left to test all those Israelites who had not experienced any of the wars in Canaan." The Bible goes on to mention three other reasons why God purposefully allowed hardship: to teach them how to do warfare (v. 2); to test their character (v. 4); and to keep wild animals from overtaking the land (Exod. 23:29). God is saying: *"I've got a bigger plan. I could give you a quick mira-*

cle. I could rid you of your irritations; but, if you don't have certain skills and character, you won't be able to maintain "Promised Land Living" anyway.[9]

The Bible also teaches that God has a timing for His glory in our lives. In John 9:1–3, we read a story that can revolutionize the way we see difficulty:

As [Jesus] went along, he saw a man blind from birth. His disciples asked him, "Rabbi, who sinned, this man or his parents, that he was born blind?" "Neither this man nor his parents sinned," said Jesus, "but this happened so that the works of God might be displayed in him."

Immediately afterwards, Jesus healed the man. And for centuries, millions of Christians have celebrated this event. However, there were a few things about this passage that bothered me for a season.

First, it seems sad that the disciples assumed the blind man's problem was a sin issue. As I just shared, there are a lot of reasons for unanswered prayer, but because many of us only know a few them, we tend to judge people and their circumstances incorrectly.

Second, it's weird to think this man lived all of his life blind, just so God could receive a glory moment. But before we jump to the strange conclusion that God did something wrong, allow me to share a few stats that might rock your world and expand your "theology of pain."

For years, researchers have noticed that people who survive traumatic events often claim *higher satisfaction in life than the general population.* When we imagine paralysis, blindness, or losing a loved one, most of us feel like curling up in a ball and listening to country music. However, people who actually suffer these impairments generally rate their lives far better than the rest of us would anticipate if *we ourselves* had those circumstances.[10] One study found that 96 percent of cancer patients felt they were healthier than the "average cancer patient."[11] Cancer patients tend to be more positive about their lives than the rest of us would imagine. The same is true with other illnesses or major disabilities. Similarly, people who survive traumatic events often claim an *increased* ability to enjoy life![12]

Now, if you're going through a traumatic period in life, I don't mean to sound as if I'm trying to minimize your pain. I'm simply asking: What if God is timing something amazing in your life? Or even more scandalous: What if our greatest pains enable our greatest pleasures?

Again, the two main ways God overcomes evil and tragedy in Scripture are: (1) He supernaturally removes it (e.g., instantaneous miracles); or (2) He creatively thwarts it to enable positive outcomes. Of course, we all hope and pray for plan A, but what if plan B is the only option that can bring us true fulfillment? What if *your* plan B was actually *God's* plan A? Or what if your tragedy becomes your greatest triumph? It sounds scary, but this was the situation Christ faced in the garden of Gethsemane when He prayed before going to the cross.

As you're about to find out, Jesus prayed one of the most power-filled prayers anyone could possibly pray—and it just might alter everything about how you relate to God. Before I share this insight, though, allow me to press the pause button and return to my family road trip for a moment.

I vividly remember my son crying out, "Daddy, don't you care?" Of course it was difficult for me because I absolutely cared, but I was shocked at how far his emotions took him. And much of it was *his own fault* for wearing that stupid swim jacket. His obsessing over his dream of the pool made his life in the car miserable.

Like my son, Eden, some of us wear our dreams way too closely. We want to get married (or stay married); we want to have kids; we want a better job, a better body, a bigger house, a better paycheck. And when these things aren't happening the way we want, we start getting the "dream disease." We become like my son, obsessing over our dreams. We wear them like sweaty swim jackets, and in time, our ambitions become toxic to our spiritual health.

When people get dream disease, five primary symptoms show up:

1. WE CONSTANTLY JABBER ARE-WE-THERE-YET PRAYERS THAT ACCOMPLISH NOTHING (MATT. 6:7).
2. WE IRRITATE OURSELVES AND EVERYONE AROUND US BECAUSE WE'RE OBSESSED WITH OUR DREAMS.
3. WE QUESTION THE PROMISES WE'VE BEEN GIVEN.
4. WE COMPLAIN AGAINST "THE DRIVER" OR WHOEVER WE PERCEIVE TO BE OBSTRUCTING OUR HAPPINESS.
5. WE OBSESS OVER CIRCUMSTANTIAL THINGS AS IF THEY'RE OUR SOURCE OF HAPPINESS.

But let's focus on symptom number four for a moment.

My son kept looking at my hands on the steering wheel, thinking, *You appear to be in control. So, why then are you not taking me to a pool?*

We have a similar tendency to rant at the person we perceive to be at the wheel of our lives—parents, bosses, pastors, politicians, ex-spouses, even God. And the more we feel out of control, the more unhappy we get. Research by psychologist and author Martin Seligman indicates that "the feeling of control" is a fundamental ingredient of happiness: "People who have a sense of control over their lives experience significant boosts in feelings of happiness, hope and elation."[13]

Gaining a sense of control has a significant clinical effect on both health and happiness. I think about this every time I pick up the twelve remote controls to my TV system. Seriously! I wonder how we can build space stations but can't figure out a simpler way to control our TV sets. Another thing I can't seem to control is the auto-correct function on my phone. It makes for many unhappy moments.

My wife, Carolyn, has a similar challenge. She often sends me unsettling texts she claims are caused by her auto-correct: "Did you pick up the LSD?" She allegedly intended to type "kids," but I wasn't convinced when I received the follow-up text: "I'm really enjoying my weed." Or, as she now claims, "week." (Now you know the *real* reason I talked about marijuana in the last chapter. Just kidding.)

However, I struggle with a similar problem. Whenever I type "haha" my autocorrect converts it to "shabaka." My Pentecostal friends think I'm texting-in-tongues. But seriously, has anyone in the history of texting ever used the word *shabaka* before? Apparently, it's the name of a Kushite pharaoh from the twenty-fifth dynasty of Egypt. But I still don't know why people would need to text about him: "Honey, could you pick up my Shabaka outfit at the cleaners before our Kushite-themed meal?" Seriously, who programmed that one into our phones?

Texting issues aside, control has a fascinating connection to happiness. That's why there are thousands of books designed to help us get in control of our health, our finances, our schedules, our kids— our lives. And we buy mass quantities of these books.

Because of the control phenomenon, there's been a huge trend in psychology circles to come up with therapies to help people "regain the feeling of control" over their lives. Yet, ironically, over the last few decades, research has shown that giving people a sense of control is one of the most destructive things we could do.

"Why?" you might ask. Quite simply, because *control is an illusion.* Human brains have an irrational "programming bug" that causes us to falsely believe it's possible for us to control more than we can.[14] For example, research shows that if we can pick our own lottery numbers, we believe our odds of winning are dramatically higher.[15] Is that rational? Certainly not! But it's why lottery games encourage participation. Casino designers exploit this mental defect by creating games that make us feel more optimistic—even though they will just as surely take our money. Another study found that if a gambler rolls the dice from his or her own hands (as opposed to someone else doing the rolling), the person will generally believe their luck increases—even though the idea is mathematically absurd.[16]

Other industries also prey upon this mental flaw by selling us the illusion of security, transformation, or being in charge. Much of modern advertising is designed to exploit our lack of control over our bodies, families, and personal security. We pay for gym memberships we don't use, home security systems we don't turn on, books on how to change that we never read, insurance policies we never benefit from. We're strangely okay with this because even though we're really just purchasing the illusion of control, it feels good to us.

You might wonder, though, why this is so destructive. If it creates a good feeling, who the heck cares—right? Who cares if security, personal change, and cure-all health foods are just illusions of power? If they make us feel good, they're worth it, aren't they? Not so.

Research also shows that when people are given a sense of control and then lose it, they're actually worse off—in terms of happiness, life-expectancy, and activeness—than people who never had a sense of control at all![17] In other words, positive self-talk, life-planning, and other simplistic health formulas can set people up for *increased* depression, lethargy, and even early death. Let me explain why.

No matter how much we do to mitigate risk and gain control, life finds a way to shatter the illusion. Nearly a million people experience unexpected life-altering events every day. We can try to prevent these traumas by wearing helmets, taking vitamin supplements, and by second-guessing our phone's auto-correct before pressing send, but healthy people still die of heart attacks. Wealthy people still die in plane crashes. Righteous people still get cancer. And no matter how much I gyrate on my home gym, I still can't get abs like Chuck Norris.

Speaking of Chuck Norris, when I was in college, a martial arts expert died right outside my house because he got stabbed by a random mugger. The victim was essentially a ninja! If there was ever a guy who should have survived a teenage thug, it was this guy. The scary revelation is this: You can spend your whole life training to be a ninja and still not be able to defend yourself.

No matter how much we try to control events in life, strange things happen. The fact is, there is far more we can't control than we can. Our potty buckets break; our honeymoons end. Our babies cry, and our employers bark. Eventually, our simplistic theologies buckle under the strain. And when our pursuits give way and our dreams crumble into the sea, we will eventually say: "I need a God who can control all of this." And He will say back: "Be still and know that I am God" (Ps. 46:10).

NOT MY WILL BUT YOURS BE DONE

I find it interesting that control is one of the first things God strips from us when we come to Him. Paul wrote, "You are not your own; you were bought at a price" (1 Cor. 6:19–20). When God reached out to Abraham, Isaac, and Jacob, the first thing He did was strip away their sense of control. He told Abraham: "Go from your country, your people and your father's household to the land I will show you" (Gen.12:1). In other words, leave every imaginable source of comfort and security and go to an unknown location. If this seems easy, simply tell your friends you're moving your entire family to "somewhere," and see what they say. If you have good friends, they'll freak out. After all, a sense of direction is fundamental to financial security.

There must have been a few moments when Abraham wondered, *How am I supposed to look forward to that kind of plan?* But God knew Abraham's wobbly scaffolding of happiness needed to be stripped away. Abraham needed a far deeper intimacy with God. And to make sure he got it, there were famines, wife-kidnappings, wars, and pregnancy problems all along the way. Just about anything Abraham thought he could control, God placed out of reach. Why? He wanted Abraham to understand that true happiness comes from God alone (Ps. 62:1). No circumstance will ever achieve this.

Impressively, in the midst of this control vacuum, Abraham built up a muscle called *faith*. He believed in a God who controls all things—a Father who has our best interests in mind, no matter how things look. And because of this wandering situation, Abraham fell upon the real keys to happiness: submission and faith. He stopped trying to get in control and instead learned to get under the control of the God who loved him.

That same sort of submission and faith is what made Christ's prayer in the garden of Gethsemane so powerful. He prayed, "Abba, Father. . . everything is possible for you. Take this cup from me" (Mark 14:36a). I think it's fascinating that, right at this point, we get to witness Christ having an "unanswered prayer." He essentially asked His Father to let Him avoid the cross. But that cup didn't pass from Him. His prayer continued: "Yet not what I will, but what You will" (Mark 14:36). Jesus made a specific request, but He followed it up with surrender.

Submission prayers don't sound sexy. The miracles they produce often take a while to manifest. Yet submission prayers are the ultimate accelerator to promotion.

One reason God doesn't always answer our prayers is that we don't end them with "but not my will." Instead, many of us pray to *get in control* rather than *under His control*. There's no true submission or reliance upon Him (2 Cor. 1:9).

I think if we prayed submission prayers more than circumstantial prayers, God would say, "Finally! You understand that submission is the true root of happiness. *Now* I can bless you with many things—without worrying that you'll start worshipping the things I'm trying to bless you with."

Don't get me wrong. It's okay to ask the Father for specific things. He loves audacious prayers! Indeed, Jesus taught an entire sermon on praying boldly (Luke 11:5–8). As Mark Batterson argues brilliantly in his book *The Circle Maker*, God loves it when we verbalize our desires (Mark 10:51). It's okay to say, "I'd love to be healed. And I'd love for it to happen right now." God loves it when we pray prayers so big that only He could make them happen (Eph. 3:20). And I love being specific enough that, when they happen, only God can get the glory.

But some Christians take God's promises to a witchcraft level. To such people, Scripture promises are incantations we can use to control God, rather than a reassurance of God's character.[18] These people still believe in a devastating myth called the Driver's-Seat Myth.

MYTH	**THE DRIVER'S-SEAT MYTH:** *Being in control is possible and will cause a lasting feeling of happiness and security.*

In the end, we don't pray to control our circumstances. Control isn't even something we can achieve apart from God (John 15:5). We pray in order to submit to the Father who controls it all. Delays may occur. Crosses may appear. Escalators may break. Dream boats may sail away. But these delays aren't necessarily a sign that God is displeased—nor the evidence of sin or a lack of faith.

If we stay submitted to God, we'll always end up in a place of greater glory. The delays can often be the greatest things that ever happen to us. And for my son on our road trip, that place of greater glory was a swimming pool.

THE PROMISED POOL OF GREATNESS

After the long drive that day, my son cannon-balled into his dream. As I saw it, that pool in Kansas City was nothing more than a big bowl of overly-chlorinated urine water, but to Eden, it was water-winged ecstasy, and his bliss was contagious. I wish you could have seen the joy on his face when he jumped in, swim jacket intact. I think everyone in that pool felt his delight.

But my son's joy wasn't merely a reaction to the cool water after a long drive. It was the fact that his father was in the pool with him, enjoying the promise alongside him. He knew, *My daddy was faithful to get me here.* And together, we had some obnoxious fun.

So if your life plan isn't working quite right, if your road trip feels hot and sweaty, or your escalator seems slow or broken, don't complain against your Father. Don't make it hard for your trip mates. And please . . . don't try to hijack the steering wheel and take short-cuts! It's only a matter of time before your tests turn into testimonies.

The more you experience God's faithfulness, the more "not my will, but Yours be done" will become the most joyful, jubilant, and exhilarating prayer you've ever prayed. You can pray that prayer right now:

Father, every dream and desire I have is secondary to Your will— which is the only true path to happiness. I trust You, no matter how it looks. Enable my faith to get my feelings in alignment with this truth. Amen.

KEY IDEAS

1. The Bible gives dozens of reasons for unanswered prayer. However, because many of us only know a few of the reasons, we tend to get confused and judge circumstances incorrectly.

2. The two main ways God overcomes evil and tragedy in Scripture are: He supernaturally removes it (e.g., instantaneous miracles) or He creatively thwarts it to enable positive outcomes.

3. It's easy to forget that God is more interested in developing both our character and faith than He is in giving us quick miracles or no trials. Unanswered prayers are one of the critical tools God uses to develop our character.

4. It's wrong to immediately interpret tragedy or unanswered prayer as evidence of sin or a lack of faith. Jesus taught His disciples to resist this instinct for numerous reasons.

5. Ironically, some of our greatest pains actually enable our greatest pleasures; our greatest pains can even create our greatest platforms.

6. When we don't give God creative freedom in answering our prayers, it often results in us complaining against God—or whoever else we perceive to be in control of our lives.

7. Control is one of the ways that fallen humanity tries to create happiness. In fact, "control" is one of the statistical predictors of happiness—which is why we spend so much money trying to pursue it.

8. Both research and Scriptures show us that control is ultimately an illusion. We falsely believe we can control far more than we actually can. This is why we are devastated and confused when we lose control.

9. Control is one of the first things God strips from us when we come to Him. He doesn't do this to be mean but rather because true control can only be found in total submission to Him.

10. Jesus showed us that the greatest prayers are not "control prayers" (God do this or that). They are "submission prayers" (God, I trust You will creatively solve this, no matter how it looks).

DISCUSSION QUESTIONS

1. What's one of the more memorable road trips you've taken? What made it so memorable?

2. According to the five reasons for unanswered prayer mentioned in this chapter, which one stuck out to you the most? Is there one you tend to gravitate towards most? Why?

3. What does the story of the blind man in John 9:1 teach us about judging people and the difficulties they face? What's a better, more compassionate way to respond to people who are suffering?

4. Have you ever had a traumatic experience that you're actually thankful for? If so, explain.

5. If traumatic experiences can actually increase our life satisfaction, how might this change the way we pray or embrace pain?

6. We discovered there are five main symptoms to Dream Disease. What is one of the dreams you are waiting for? Which of these five symptoms are you most likely to experience?

7. Is there an area of your life that you'd like to have more control over? If so, what?

8. Why do you think control makes us feel so good? What is one area where you would like to have an extra amount of it (finances, physical body, vacation planning, home security, job security) and why? How have you seen other people seek control?

9. Why do you think God wants to break us away from the illusion of control? What's an example of control gone bad?

10. If "submission prayers" give God more creative freedom, how might this be a good thing?

3

THE DAY ALL MY DREAMS CAME TRUE, AND I HATED IT

What If Your Prayers Reveal Your Pathologies?

Y
ou don't even know what the heck you want. You may not want to admit it—yet—but it's true. Both science and Scripture provide plenty of evidence showing that our desires change faster than we think. And by the end of this chapter, the evidence may permanently change the types of prayers you pray—for the better.

"But I know what I want in life!" you say, "And I know how to pray!"

If that's you, here's a quick story to slap your denial in the face.

A few years back, I found the "dream property" for our church. It was gorgeous—flowing with milk and honey, so to speak. I dragged my kids on prayer walks around it every week. I anointed the building with oil. I did every spooky thing a Christian could possibly do to "claim the territory" for God. I even Jericho-marched it. The only thing I didn't do was blow a shofar over it. And why? After hosing it down with my spiritual prowess, I was afraid the walls might actually crumble. (After all, I'd hate to get to heaven and hear God say, "Sorry, Pete. You weren't specific enough! You did a Jericho march, and I gave a Jericho answer!" So, I always try to be specific with God: no shofar, no walls fall, right?)

But here's the twist to my story. After spending a lot of money having appraisers and other experts evaluate the property, it turned out the land was also flowing with soil contamination. Anyone who purchased the property would be on the hook for unlimited lawsuits. In fact, there was a class-action suit being drafted against the property during the very moments I was prayer-walking it. Had we bought that property, it would have been a long-term disaster for our church.

Like I mentioned in the introduction, many of our dreams are *Titanic* dreams. There are things that only God knows, and after dozens of experiences like this, I've learned to give God a lot more creative freedom when it comes to my prayers.

Here's another reason to give God creative license: *You don't even know what makes you happy.* Every week I meet people who are pouring a heroic amount of energy into doctoring a "perfect circumstance"—only to discover their dreams are changing.

As researchers have studied happiness and how we achieve it, they've found that humans are rather fickle. For example, surveys show that most Americans imagine that "life in California is happier," but no reliable statistical evidence exists to show that Californians are actually happier than anyone else.[19] Part of the reason for this misperception is that when people imagine themselves in the Golden State, they imagine themselves hanging out at the beach with movie stars every day. In reality, of course, most of us would be gridlocked somewhere on California's overcrowded freeways trying to get to our third job—just to afford a grungy apartment that would rent for one-fourth the price of a much larger apartment in Minnesota, Texas, or Tennessee.[20]

Don't get me wrong. When I meet people who've lived in many cities, I often ask them, "What was your favorite city?" They always have a favorite. They usually give me superficial reasons for why they like it such as the weather, or the lifestyle, etc. But nine times out of ten, that same city was the place where they had the largest amount of purpose and life-giving friendships—two of the largest predictors of happiness. Thus, some geographical locations can definitely hold a prominent place in our hearts, but not for the reasons we often imagine.

Research also shows that when people imagine the future, they tend to hang the majority of their "predicted future happiness" on singular concerns like *Did I get married?* to the exclusion of other important factors like *How do I handle my new spouse's debts, doubts, and drinking problems?* In other words, when we romanticize our narrow fantasies of the future, we generally leave out significant details like, "my dream house has more square footage to clean."[21]

To illustrate this, allow me tell you about a time when all my dreams came true, and I hated it. By the end of my story, I hope you will have a more sophisticated framework for discerning God's will. We'll begin with another myth:

THE OVERSIMPLIFICATION MYTH:
Promotion will make my life easier or happier.[22]

I had the privilege of working for two great senior pastors before I became one. But, like most young punks, I secretly thought, *Perhaps I could do everything better.* As a lowly youth pastor, I also remember thinking, *Ugh! I wish I could make that decision instead!* or, *If only people knew what I know. If I could control that budget or this hiring decision, revival would completely fall upon this organization.* Don't get me wrong: I wasn't a total idiot (notice the qualifier, *total*), but it always seemed like my previous bosses and leaders had a lot more freedom, more money, and more authority than I did.

Over the years, I've noticed that many people are dominated by the idea that life's greatest opportunities are being wasted on people who don't know what they're doing. We've all thought so at some point. Perhaps you're an athlete waiting for your dimwit coach to wise up and put you in the game. You're a musician waiting for the recording industry to get a clue about your talent. You're the bridesmaid, not the bride. So, you think, *When will the world wake up to my greatness? And why are there so many idiots out there who seem to squander their opportunities?*

Fast-forward a few years. Against all odds I became the senior pastor of the same church in Wisconsin where I had served as a youth pastor. I'll never forget my first day, sitting in the glorious office behind my huge desk. I put both palms down, and with my chin held high, I majestically looked out of my executive window. I could feel it: I was about to change the whole freaking world. I could hear the crowds chanting: "Yes, you can! Yes, you can!" The soundtrack from the movie *Gladiator* played in my head. But over the next few months, I realized that nobody else could hear what I heard. Instead, they heard something more like the theme song from the sitcom *The Office.*

The moment I became senior pastor, it seemed like the entire church secretly conspired to fight about everything. Staff members emerged from dark crevices to ask me about my budgeting motives. Suddenly, it was mandatory that I attend strange events like kindergarten graduation ceremonies. (Let's be honest: do kindergartners *really* need a graduation?)

One exasperated Sunday morning, I announced: "Church, I could get a lot more work done if all of you would stop sinning!" But did they listen? No. Instead, they embroiled me in Sister So-and-So's controversial theology of breast feeding. *Does the Bible even address this?* I wondered. But, nobody listened to me. Despite all my new-found authority, my new responsibilities felt like eating pancakes and syrup with my bare hands—inefficient and messy.

Although I had ten times the budget to manage, I had fifty times the number of people begging me for money. Oh yes, my authority was greater, but the number of people scrutinizing my decisions and soaking up my time was greater times ten. As King Solomon once said, "Better one handful with tranquility than two handfuls with toil and chasing after the wind" (Eccl. 4:6). Quite simply, sometimes less is more.

The stunning irony of my promotion was this: Now that I finally had the authority to do what I wanted, I didn't even have the time to enjoy the authority I possessed! I had to delegate most of it away—*to my youth pastor!* It was mind-numbingly frustrating. I felt compelled to beg forgiveness from all of my former leaders.

Around that same time, I read a John Maxwell leadership book, in which he wrote, "The greatest fallacy of leadership is that a higher level of promotion will make your life simpler."[23]

"What?" I shouted, as I threw the book across the room. "But I have a secretary and a glorious desk now. These things are supposed make my life simpler!"

Deep down, we all believe life should be simpler, don't we? When I was a kid, for example, the refrigerator magically stocked itself with food. Hot cocoa would randomly appear with marshmallows after I played in the snow—often with cookies to the side. It was a magically simpler world. I had never heard of cars needing "oil changes." Don't they just go wherever you need them to?

About the time I moved out of my parent's house, it seemed like my whole world suddenly became problematic. It was almost as if the federation of secret servant monkeys suddenly went on strike. Every dream seemed to detour through an infuriating bog of insurance decisions, deadlines, and endless hordes of crazy-stupid people with opinions opposite of mine.

THE TWO REACTIONS WHEN OUR DREAMS GET BOGGED

When your feet start sinking in this bog of complexity, you'll likely take one of two positions:

1. THE EVERYTHING-IS-WRONG WORLDVIEW.

"I shouldn't have to 'take off my shoes' in order to change my pants!" you declare, as you trip wildly across your bedroom floor. Life should "just work." And when our idealism gets tangled in reality, we shout, "Why is everything so wrong?" Then there's the alternative worldview.

2. THE MY-EXPECTATIONS-OF-THE-WORLD-ARE-STUPID-AND-INACCURATE WORLDVIEW.

This position requires more humility, of course. After all, you may need to apologize to a long list of former bosses, leaders, and parents. The good news, though, is that humble pie is low in calories and high in nutrition, and God gives a disproportionate amount of grace to those who eat it (1 Peter 5:5–6).

Over the years, I've made it to a lot of milestones that I was certain would bring me "lasting happiness." For years, I falsely believed the classic pastor myth that more church attendees would

HAPPINESS ISN'T A CIRCUMSTANCE. IT'S A LIVING BEING— YOUR HEAVENLY FATHER.

make me happy. Or that perhaps an internationally selling book would do it. But nothing lasted. No matter how many attendance records we broke, it never brought lasting happiness.

Ironically, research generally shows that happiness tends to decline as a person's salary increases. Wealthy people tend to worry more than the general population and experience more daily anger.[24] Yet, despite reading numerous studies like this, I still thought, *Maybe I'll be the exception. At least give me the chance to test this out for myself!*

To return to our "pantiful" metaphor: We're not stupid enough to take off our skinny jeans while we still have our shoes on but how about jogging pants? "Allow me to try!" we cry. "I think it will work for me!" But then, as you weep in your undies, shoes firmly wedged in your self-made Chinese finger trap, you ask yourself, *When will I learn?*

"When" is a good question, my friend, because that moment of learning can start right now.

Happiness researcher, Sonja Lyubomirsky points out that "circumstances and situations only account for about a 10 percent variance in happiness."[25] Wealth, beauty, health, and marital status only affect life-satisfaction by about 10 percent!

So what accounts for the rest? As you read on, I promise to give lots of fascinating clues, but allow me to cut to the chase with one simple truth: *There will never be a circumstance that satisfies you.* Here's why: "[Your] soul finds rest in God" (Ps. 62:1). Happiness isn't a circumstance. It's a living being—your heavenly Father.

With a church full of thousands of twenty-to-fiftysomethings, I hear the following sequence of prayers on a weekly basis:

- *"Lord I want to be married;"*
- which progresses to, *"Lord, help me stay married."*
- Then, *"Lord, help me have kids,"*
- followed by, *"Help my kids sleep through the night."*
- Then, *"Help my lazy kids wake up and help,"*
- Followed by, *"Help me to sleep and not kill my spouse and teenagers."*
- After that, *"Help my spouse and adult kids not kill me."*

It's an ironic, vicious cycle in which our blessings become our curses. So don't condemn yourself to a lifestyle of insatiable consumption. The treadmill of elusive circumstantial happiness is cruel. It will hijack your prayer life, arrest your relationship with God, and ultimately cause you to miss the fact that happiness is a spiritual problem—not a circumstantial problem. In fact, this brings up our fourth myth:

THE CALIFORNIA MYTH:
Promotion is a circumstantial or locational problem.

Recently, I was reading an autobiography of one of the richest and most powerful men ever to walk the earth. His book is called Ecclesiastes, and his name is King Solomon. Despite his endless wealth and never ending supply of lovely spouses, he, too, championed the earth-shattering idea that enjoyment operates independently of circumstances. Ecclesiastes 6:1–2 says:

I have seen another evil under the sun, and it weighs heavily on mankind: God gives some people wealth, possessions and honor, so that they lack nothing their hearts desire, but God does not grant them the ability to enjoy them.

In other words, enjoyment is a gift that comes *exclusively* from God, and this gift operates independently of our circumstances. This is why even rich people commit suicide, gorgeous celebrities partner swap, and people in Beverly Hills still murder each other.

But the next question is this: Why would God prevent people from enjoying something? Is He mean or cruel? Ironically, the exact opposite is true.

FRIENDS WITH A ROCK STAR

It's important to understand that God created everything for our pleasure. Think about it. This is the God who created taste buds. He created the color spectrum and over 400,000 varieties of flowers. He created us with the ability to weep tears of joy after listening to vibrations of sound. He made textures, and hormones like adrenaline. And He intended all of these things to inspire worship from our hearts. He fashioned this astounding world and called it "good" (Gen. 1:9, 12, 18, 21, 25)—even "*very* good" (Gen. 1:31, emphasis mine).

As a father myself, I think it's delirious fun to introduce my kids to the gifts of life. I delighted in watching my kids taste ice cream for the first time. I loved teaching them how to form their first snowball, catch their first lightning bug, or eat their first all-potato-chip breakfast.

Notice in that list, though, I didn't say "I delighted in giving them heroine or crack cocaine" (although some of you may be thinking the potato chip breakfast is close). Like any good father, I won't give my children experiences I know will destroy them. Which is the same reason God doesn't give everyone equal freedom to enjoy life. Freedom is a privilege that must be earned.

For example, if people have a diseased sense of priority—if they find their primary fulfillment in created things instead of their Creator—all of these sensations are just a distraction. They can even destroy our potential. So if God has to temporarily rob you of enjoyment to wake you up, so be it. What kind of loving Father would He be if He enabled us to have pleasures that distracted us from our greatest pathologies?

After I gave my heart to Christ, everything changed. Oceans were more beautiful. Tacos were tastier. Christmas was dreamier. Even *sacrifice* became fun! And it was more than fun; it became relational.

Sunsets, stars, and sailfish weren't merely breathtaking objects that glowed, twinkled, and jumped around me. They were love letters from my Creator to me. On top of my natural enjoyment of those things, I suddenly had the additional pleasure of worshipping the One who created them! It's like being best friends with your favorite rock star who gives you a private concert and interview whenever you want it. How could you ever go back to merely listening to impersonal songs on a playlist?

I realize that my conversion experience was a bit more dramatic than most,[26] but it felt like God flipped on a switch and said, "Finally! I can give him a new level of pleasure without fear that he will enslave himself—or worship the things I'm blessing him with."[27]

Now, if you're anything like me, you're thinking, *Okay, Peter. That sounds like great poetry, but how do I know if God has "turned on" my enjoyment switch?* Indeed, there's lots of evidence to suggest that God possesses such a switch!

Consider this. If you go to church regularly you are 22 percent less likely to be clinically depressed,[28] you're more likely to have orgasms and high levels of sexual satisfaction,[29] you're more likely to manage your life better,[30] manage your time better,[31] you're more likely to complete degrees[32] and achieve other academic milestones,[33] and you'll likely have increased "mental well-being."[34] As if these weren't enough, regular church attendees live significantly longer than the general population[35]—seven to fourteen years longer than nonreligious people![36] Even stranger, merely believing in the value of church attendance isn't enough. Only those who actually attend church events regularly experience many of these benefits—and some of the benefits are shown to increase with more frequent attendance.

For years, secular researchers looked at these studies and asked: Are these benefits unique to church-goers? Could we create a "church-like" experience for people who don't believe in God and achieve the same results? One study suggests, no. When you compare "secular support groups" with "faith-based" groups, Judeo-Christian groups strangely seem to have a monopoly on certain protective factors.[37]

All I'm suggesting is this: What if the Bible is true? What if our pleasure and enjoyment really are a spiritual issue rather than a circumstantial issue? What if God cranks up our enjoyment and pleasure when we put Him first? What if God is so aware of our idolatrous tendencies that He dials back our enjoyment as a protective mechanism—lest we become the proverbial moth attracted to the flame?

"But Peter," you say, "my church is completely dead! There's no way it could generate those statistical results."

If that's you, I can empathize with that. There are a million churches I would *not* want to go to. But the research is nonetheless true. Committed church-goers have a statistical advantage in living life—not to mention hanging around for more of it. Even if you don't fully believe in God, the research alone suggests that you owe it to yourself to start looking for a church. (And if you need a few tips in finding a good church, check out this endnote.[38] There are a few statistical predictors of church happiness tucked in that note too.)

But here's the biggest problem you need to consider. Many of you probably think, *Peter, I already believe what you're saying*— but the problem is, you actually don't! You think to yourself, *Yeah, yeah. Money doesn't buy happiness . . . blah, blah, blah*, or, *I already know that "My soul finds rest in God alone"* (Ps. 62:1). Yet, for many of us, this is the very reason God needs to break our escalators: You're in total denial about how you actually pursue happiness.

So, allow me to give you a self-test to see if you're living in denial. As I hinted at the beginning of this chapter, your prayers reveal your pathologies. So, are you ready?

YOUR PRAYERS—THE GREAT SELF-TEST

If you're praying more for circumstantial things than for character, you're out of sync with God. If we really believed enjoyment comes from God more than our circumstances—if we really believed "our souls find rest in God" (Ps. 62:1)—we wouldn't waste so much time asking for circumstantial things (Matt. 6:7, 25). We'd be asking for more of Him and His character. I'll tell you why.

Opportunity and promotion have never been a problem for God. He could snap His fingers and quadruple your opportunities and income today (1 Sam. 2:7). In fact, that's one of the main points of the Old Testament book, First Samuel.[39] If you've got adequate character, God's promotion will stalk you—even if you're hidden in a field like David. This truth is also echoed in the story of King Nebuchadnezzar.

Nebuchadnezzar was one of the most powerful kings in history. He started to believe that he was pretty awesome at orchestrating

IF YOU'RE PRAYING MORE FOR CIRCUMSTANTIAL THINGS THAN FOR CHARACTER, YOU'RE OUT OF SYNC WITH GOD.

the circumstances of his life and kingdom. Out of mercy, God gave Nebuchadnezzar a dream to remind him that *only* God has the power to create happiness, peace, and security. But, despite this warning, the king became full of himself. So finally the prophetic consequence came forth: "You will be driven away from people and will live with the wild animals . . . until you acknowledge that the Most High is sovereign over all kingdoms on earth and gives them to anyone he wishes" (Dan. 4:25).

But what are the "kingdoms on earth"? I suppose it could be a church, a business, or anything else God has entrusted to us—kids, salaries, inheritances. God is more than willing to upgrade each of these stewardships in direct proportion to our character. Indeed, He *longs* to do so, provided we don't get arrogant or idolatrous like Nebuchadnezzar (Dan. 4:30).

So what happened to Nebuchadnezzar? Exactly as God had promised, the king suddenly lost his mind. He went crazy for seven years. He wandered out of the palace into the countryside and ate grass like a cow. And just like God promised, after seven years of madness, Nebuchadnezzar woke up again—except this time he had more appreciation for the power of God to affect his circumstances. Almost equally incredible is that the people received Nebuchadnezzar back as king. Only God could take a person who messed up so completely and give him credibility again.

It's a fascinating story, but here's the point: Promoting people has never been a problem for God. Hear me, though, promotion and character are different things. Character makes you promotable. Without it, you'll never get the promotion. That's why the ultimate test is this: Do you pray more for promotability or for promotion?

For example, instead of praying "God, give me a spouse," you should pray "Give me character that makes me worthy of a spouse." Instead of praying "God give me this particular job or that opportunity," pray "Lord, give me a connection to You that would sustain me through such an opportunity!" Do you see the difference?

Don't misunderstand me. Go ahead and ask God for anything. Jesus preached an entire sermon on how to pray bold prayers (Luke 11:5–13). I even think you should ask God for *huge* specific things so that when He answers, only He can get the glory.

Like I shared in chapter 1, God wants to restore our capacity to dream, to look into our futures and speak things into existence with awe-inspiring creativity. But since we may not fully grasp what God wants for us, when you pray, it's still crucial to add "not my will but Yours be done." Always let submission prayers be the joyful climax. After all, the place of submission is the happiest place in the universe. Joy is not a location or circumstance; it's a position of heart.

Prayer is far more than *supplication* (asking God for things). It's meant to be a conversation dominated with adoration and thanksgiving. Even when we ask for things—and we *should*—our requests should be dominated with character appeals such as "lead us not into temptation." Why? "Because your Father knows what you need before you ask him" (Matt. 6:8). And "My God will meet all your needs according to his glorious riches in Christ Jesus" (Phil. 4:19).

If we spend all our time "asking God for things" (a.k.a., the Supplication Syndrome), it's actually a sign that we're "Fatherless" and dominated by paganism (see Matt. 6:7, 32). Imagine if every time you saw one of your loved ones, you asked him or her for something and said nothing else. I can pretty much promise you that's not a healthy relationship. The same is true for your relationship with God.

The craziness of King Nebuchadnezzar is a fitting metaphor for many of us. We're crazily pursuing the perfect circumstances. We're so busy looking for greener grass that, like the mad king, our hair looks like eagle feathers. Our fingernails are creepy-long, and we babble the same circumstantial prayers while grass tumbles off our lips.

At some point, we need to look to heaven and proclaim: "God, You love me so much that you've purposefully been protecting me from the very things I've been panting for. You are sovereign over the kingdoms of people. And like a good Father, You've been holding back my inheritance until I'm ready to use it wisely (Dan. 4:34–35). So please work into my life what pleases You (Heb. 13:21)."

The real miracle in King Nebuchadnezzar's story is that God completely restored him to power again. Just think, God can take a crazy man and turn him *back into a king*. So if you wake up naked in a field someday with grass clippings all over your face, don't freak out. God isn't done with you.

Here's one last reason we want to believe that "happiness is a circumstantial problem" instead of a character problem. As long as the problem is "out there" (e.g., "The problem is my boss, spouse, church, kids, government—anyone but me!"), then we can absolve ourselves of responsibility. It's called the Blame Game. People have been playing it since the garden of Eden (Gen. 3:12–13), but listen to me, loved ones, it only leads to shame and discontentment.

Yes, God may still be calling you to California, but if your heart's right you won't be swayed by myths that such moves will make your life happier or simpler. And when you pray, you won't waste your time Jericho-marching around toxic waste dumps. No matter where you live, you'll look at the sunset and say, "Thanks God for making all this for me. I love You." And God will say back, "You ain't seen nothing yet!"

Lord, there is no location or circumstance that will satisfy me. Only Your presence and a fresh deposit of Your Holy Spirit can satisfy me. Heavenly Father, deliver us from the evil myths that cloud our judgment and crowd out the wonderful relationship that You're calling us to.

KEY IDEAS

1. Research shows that when we imagine the future, we leave out many important details, both good and bad.

2. We falsely imagine happiness to be found in places where, statistically speaking, it doesn't necessarily exist.

3. Promotion doesn't necessarily make our lives happier or simpler.

4. There will never be a circumstance that will satisfy you. Happiness isn't a circumstance. It's a living being, your heavenly Father. Therefore, happiness is a spiritual problem, not a circumstantial problem.

5. Enjoyment is a gift that comes exclusively from God, and this gift operates independently of our circumstances (Eccl. 6).

6. Consistent church attendees enjoy a long list of positive benefits the general population doesn't enjoy. These benefits have fascinated researchers for decades.

7. God will hold back enjoyment and blessings until He knows you won't worship those blessings. He does this out of love, to prevent you from a deeper disaster: separation from Him.

8. Your prayers reveal your pathologies. If you are praying for circumstantial things more than character, you're most likely out of sync with God.

9. When you pray, always add "not my will but yours be done." After all, the place of submission is the happiest place in the universe. Joy is not a location or circumstance; it's a position of heart.

10. If we waste our time asking God for things (a.k.a., the Supplication Syndrome), it's actually a sign that we're "fatherless" and dominated by paganism (Matt. 6:7, 32).

DISCUSSION QUESTIONS

1. Have you ever idealized the future, and when you got there, it wasn't as wonderful as you expected? Or have your qualifications for happiness ever changed with time? If so, explain.

2. Can you think of any other examples of "promotion" that make our lives more complex? Or can you think of an "answer to prayer" that made your life more difficult? How might this change the way you think about promotion?

3. What are some of the common things people condition their happiness on? What are some of the circumstances that you have a tendency to idealize?

4. Can you think of a parenting situation in which it would be wise to hold back kids or teens from "enjoyment"? Can you think of any circumstances where God may do the same for us?

5. I pointed out over a half dozen benefits for people who attend church regularly (from life-expectancy to depression). Which of these studies or benefits stuck out to you the most? Why?

6. Why do you think these benefits apply only to those who actually attend church, not to those who merely believe church attendance is a good idea? In other words, what is it about church attendance that makes the difference?

7. In light of these benefits, church attendance seems wise. Yet many people struggle with going to church. Why do you think this is?

8. What circumstantial thing are you most inclined to pray for? What's the circumstance you're most inclined to worry about?

9. How might the concepts of "praying for promotability more than promotion" or "character more than circumstances" change the way you pray (for the circumstantial thing you previously mentioned)?

10. Most people think of prayer only as "asking God for things." But what are some of the other disciplines and activities that occur in prayer? How do you pray?

HOW TO TALK
A MANLY MAN INTO
CIRCUMCISION

What If Seeking Promotion Is the Ultimate Distraction from Living Promotably?

A few years back, I saw a commercial for a social anxiety drug. As the voiceover guy began listing the side effects near the end of the commercial, he suddenly mentioned: "[This drug] can cause chronic diarrhea."

What? I wondered. *It will solve your social anxiety but cause chronic diarrhea?*

Hmmm. That does not strike me as an improvement. I mean, if there was ever a symptom that would *create* social anxiety for me, it would be chronic diarrhea—especially since I'm a public speaker. (Sorry if that's TMI.)

As the commercial rolled on, though, it showed people swinging on swings, riding bikes, playing football, doing ballet—which are the precise hobbies I would avoid if there was even the slightest possibility of a diarrhea hit. Truth be told, I wouldn't do ballet either way, but after that side-effect warning, the rest of the commercial turned into a horror film. With every passing image, I felt like shouting, "Why are you bending over to snap a football? You dork! Shouldn't you be hanging out near a bathroom?"

I suppose, however, if the drug works, we won't care about the side effects:

"Dude! [gag] What did you do?"

"Hey . . . it's all good! Let's just keep riding our bikes! I'm not bothered by this stuff anymore. Let's be social!"

I'd be shocked if that commercial sold a whole lot of pills. It allegedly solves one problem while creating a more explosive one (in my opinion). Yet it's a great metaphor for how a lot of people live.

The world is constantly trying to sell us solutions that don't solve our problems. We're bombarded with shortcuts to happiness that have appalling side effects—or at the very least, don't solve our core problem. We're now exposed to more than 5,000 advertisements a day, all of which are designed to make us think, *My life would be better if I had or did [fill-in-the-blank]*. So it's no wonder we're confused, impatient, and feeling passed-by.

As a pastor, I watch a lot of people get lured into taking shortcuts to their dreams: They marry a "fixer-upper." They get into foolish debt. They switch jobs, churches, and spouses. And in the effort to "upgrade their lives" they accomplish the exact opposite.

Our brains are actually quite similar to a faulty software operating system that hackers can exploit. As I'm about to show, our brains are preprogrammed to make illogical decisions when it comes to our happiness. Marketing psychologists are well aware of our vulnerabilities, and they utilize all kinds of tricks to turn us into consumers.

Did you know, for example, that if a real estate agent shows you a terrible house before a nice house, you're statistically more likely to put an offer on the nice house? Sales Psychology 101 states that an agent should always show consumers a "more extreme" product before showing them the one the sales person actually thinks they will buy. Also, people will more likely make a larger donation if they're offered a tough donation option first: "Instead of donating $5,000, would you be open to $50?" Or "Dump ice-water over your head or donate a dollar?"

These might seem to be harmless little brain glitches, but imagine how this defect could play out with a bigger decision. Let's say, you just got out of a terrible dating relationship and then into a mediocre one. Your brain is more likely to think your second option is "the One" even if that person is dramatically below average simply by virtue of comparison.

Another proven trick is to limit a consumer's options. A lot of businesses won't sell more than two types of the same kind of product anymore, unless there's a distinct difference in its application or purpose. Here's why: When a seller gives a consumer two or more good options, it will decrease sales by at least 24 percent! It's because human beings tend to freeze up and delay decisions when they have too many good options.[40]

Another way that sales psychologists hack your brain is by "sales pricing." Say you're looking for your dream television. You find one for $800, but you just found out that, unfortunately, last week it was on sale for $600. You missed the sale. But you discover a $1,000 television is marked down to $800—"on sale!" Studies show that people will buy the "recently marked down" TV almost every time, even if the competing television set is basically the identical model![41] In other words, humans have a "bandwagon impulse." The perception of shifting value will generally override our ability to weigh the more obvious criteria.

But wait a second, you wonder. *The televisions are identical, yet we'll routinely choose the one over the other?*

Exactly! It's totally illogical—which is also why people regularly abandon stock in perfectly good companies, right before the stock skyrockets. Psychology shows that human decision-making is very much illogical. But it is *predictably* illogical—which is why we're exploring these myths of promotion.

Perhaps you're thinking, *A bad television decision won't make or break my life.* That's true. Chances are, though, you're about to make a more significant decision: taking a new job, finding a different church, moving to another city, or making a significant relationship change. So beware that your brain can be hacked into making illogical decisions. The more you're aware of the myths we're talking about, the more you can avoid betting your life on fool's gold.

Another mental lapse that afflicts people is the "perception of least resistance." We convince ourselves that one path is easier than another, and we fixate on details that confirm our bias.[42] For example, there are many unhappy married people who think, *It'd be easier to start from scratch with another person than it would be to work it out with my current spouse.* Of course, this is almost never true emotionally, economically, or relationally. Like the California Myth in the previous chapter, we tend to leave out the mundane details when we romanticize the future. People don't think about how complicated it is to divide assets, friendships, and kids. There's an entire grieving process attached to each of these. People also don't think about the grief of watching your ex-partner find new romance. They don't think about future holidays. They don't expect to grieve "time lost." And most of all, they don't expect that someday they may repeat the exact same fight with a future "dream spouse." So . . . perhaps . . . working it out would be easier after all.

When we're anxious and feeling entitled, we ignore all sorts of details and confidently cry out, "Chronic diarrhea is worth it!" But how will you feel, in the middle of your tragic ballet class, when "it" hits you? Or you get that breakaway run in football and you "explode" across the field?

Now that I've thoroughly motivated you (and ruined your love for ballet), I want to introduce two more myths of promotion. The first of these is the Talent Myth:

THE TALENT MYTH:
An exceedingly developed talent is the primary ingredient that qualifies me for promotion—more than character, experience, perseverance, loyalty, or leadership.

Having a church full of twentysomethings, I encounter this myth frequently. As they enter the "real world," they realize quickly that talented people aren't always given the most opportunities or promotions. When I was younger this seemed unfair to me too. But thankfully, God shattered this myth in me before I did something stupid.

I entered into full-time ministry a lot younger than most people. By the time I was twenty-nine, I had already written nearly a thousand sermons. However, at the time, I wasn't getting a lot of speaking opportunities outside of my church. Part of the reason was that before planting Substance Church I had pastored a small-town church in rural Wisconsin, and it didn't fit the mold for "success" as a pastor. I was told, "If you want to write books or speak at conferences, you've got to have the three B's: a *big* church, that's *blowing up*, and is near the *Bible Belt*." But the only B's we had in our small Wisconsin town were beer bellies, Brewers, and boredom. So, over the years, I felt like I was living in the land of no opportunity.

During that time, I went to a pastor's conference. As I listened to the speakers I found myself getting really mad because they were so lame! I kept thinking, *Why are these duffers getting opportunities like this? Why do I feel like I'm the only one who's not enjoying this?*

It seemed like they had stage time, not because they were truly talented or insightful, but because of where they lived and who they knew. To be totally honest, of course, I was also mad because I was jealous. I wasn't getting any invites to speak at conferences, and yet, at the time, I was pretty stinkin' incredible (at least my wife and mom thought so). Looking back now, even though I had a thousand sermons under my belt, I was still a "solid mediocre" speaker. Still, at the very least, I knew I could edge out most of the dudes who spoke at that conference.

Have you ever felt this way before? C'mon! Confess it! You know, you're kind of a "big deal." As you sang in the shower this morning, you thought, *Wow, I've really got some sizzle!* As you beat your grandma at ping pong the other night, you imagined, *I could've gone pro at this!* And as grandma got you a victory snack, you sat back and imagined the life you almost had.

We've all been in the position where we wondered, *Why did he make the team and I didn't? Why did she get promoted and I didn't?*

That was the dialogue going on in my head as I sat in the audience at that pastor's conference when suddenly, I felt the Holy Spirit rebuke me. It wasn't an audible voice but a clear impression saying, *Peter, do you really think that "opportunity" is a problem for Me? Do you really think anyone or anything could stand in the way of Me promoting you?* And right after this reprimand exploded across my heart, I sensed God's gentle Spirit continue, *Peter, your talent could handle this platform any day of the week, but your character and leadership aren't even remotely ready!*

As I sat there, my next thought was, *Is this my over-active imagination telling me this?* I found myself wanting to debate the impression. It was completely contrary to my prevailing emotions.

TALENT, STRENGTH, AND SKILL ARE NOT THE RAREST COMMODITIES; GOD IS LOOKING FOR PERSEVERANCE, LOYALTY, AND CONTINUAL TRUST—TRAITS THAT ARE MUCH HARDER TO FIND.

When I got back to the hotel that night, my mind still wrestled with the thought: *Are my expectations completely out of sync with God? Was the timeline I drafted up for my life completely artificial or ego-driven?*

That night, I started reading one of the best books in the Bible on promotion: 1 Samuel. It's filled with leadership contrasts: Hannah vs. Peninnah, Eli vs. Samuel, David vs. Goliath, Saul vs. David. But in reality, it's about people vs. God.

First Samuel brims with lessons on promotability—with illustrations about how God blesses character over talent. If I could summarize 1 and 2 Samuel in a few sentences, it would be this: Opportunity has never been God's problem; the faithfulness and integrity of His leaders have always been the showstoppers. A second theme could be this: Talent, strength, and skill are not the rarest commodities; God is looking for perseverance, loyalty, and continual trust—traits that are much harder to find.

As the verses in 1 Samuel 2:7, 9 state, "The LORD sends poverty and wealth; he humbles and he exalts. . . . It is not by strength that one prevails." Unfortunately, we see person after person in the Bible fail their tests. Even when Samuel was looking for the next king of Israel, the Spirit of God passed over at least seven others before pointing out the future King David, hidden in a field (1 Sam. 16:11).

As I sat in my hotel room that night, I realized God's rebuke was dead-on. I remember making this prayerful commitment:

God, from now on, I'm not going to pray for platform opportunities;

75

I'm going to pray for character. From now on, I'm not going to pray for promotion but rather, promotability. Lord, you don't need talent. You need character. You need people like David who will seek after your own heart.

That night, I also made a decision to stop griping about who deserves which opportunities. Once I fully entrusted promotions and platforms to God, I honestly became a kinder and more teachable person.

So listen to me, loved ones. God can snap His fingers and make any one of us wealthy or successful. And over your lifetime, you'll watch Him do the reverse too. He can answer every one of our circumstantial prayers. That's the easy part. In fact, He'd love to be able to grant your every wish. But because He also *loves* you, He's going to make sure you have the character, the perseverance, and the leadership to handle your opportunities. Many of the promotions we pine after would either destroy us or hinder a future blessing God is creating for us. He truly wants to fulfill many of your dreams. The question is, does your soul have the integrity necessary to support the weight of those dreams? Now just in case you're thickheaded like me, allow me to give you one more proof that promotability is a far better focus than promotion.

"GOD, PLEASE LET ME WIN THE LOTTERY"

Have you ever asked God to let you win the lottery? Be honest. You got that one piece of junk mail saying, "You're a winner!" And as you looked in the mirror with wide nostrils, you thought, *Dog-gonnit, I am a winner, aren't I?*

A moment later, of course, you realized that you *might* be a winner. You're eligible to win either a new set of steak knives or the ten-million-dollar prize. And that's when you prayed, "Lord, if you help me win the ten million, I promise to [fill-in-the-blank]." Even if you didn't recognize the foolishness of such a prayer at the time, as you read the next paragraph, I think you will.

People who win the lottery tend to have dramatically increased odds of getting divorced, kidnapped, murdered, and sued. They're inclined to have higher rates of depression, suicide, and bankruptcy. In fact, roughly 70 percent of lottery winners lose *all* of their money within a few years after winning it.[43] And in what might be considered the greatest irony of all, numerous studies found that the more money you win, the more likely you are to go bankrupt![44] Why? Because winning the lottery doesn't change your stewardship problems.

If you were smart with money, you wouldn't be playing the lottery in the first place.[45] As the Scriptures say, "Wealth gained hastily will dwindle, but whoever gathers little by little will increase it" (Prov.13:11, ESV). The same is usually true with all big promotions or windfall gains, which leads us to the sixth myth:

THE POT-OF-GOLD MYTH:
A golden opportunity, big promotion, or dazzling relationship will improve my character.

When our dreams aren't coming true on the schedule we expect, many of us start playing the "lottery": we settle for a good-looking, "fixer-upper spouse" or we make the cross country move for a job that *might* pan out. Rather than working on our character or our promotability, we start looking for "circumstantial shortcuts"—the pot of gold, the opportunity that will magically solve everything. Why live on a budget, for example, when you can simply look for a higher paying job? Or why become a better employee, when you can simply shop for a better boss? Why not *get* a better spouse instead of *be* a better spouse? You get the idea.

So here's a more reliable truth: Opportunity doesn't change your character; it magnifies and reveals it.

Before you won the lottery and went bankrupt, no one knew you were an idiot with your money. Now, you're another moral tale for bloggers, whose story will be retold every time there's a new lottery winner.

Your sexual problems weren't newsworthy until you got that new platform: You won the job; you got the big gig. You finally found the hot Christian spouse (who also happens to have a drinking problem), and you gave birth to triplets.

Unfortunately, when we seek promotions that God isn't giving to us, we just fail bigger. Premature promotions can create remarkable demotions. Even worse, we can become stuck in a never-ending search for better circumstances rather than living a lifestyle worthy of better circumstances.

People do this with relationships all the time. I talk to a lot of single men who think unrealistically, *If I truly find "the one," my eyes will never wander!* Or single women hope for a dream spouse who will change their contentment issues. Yet, if anything, the opposite is true. Finding "the one" challenges your character more. Marriage and intimacy will show what you're really made of.

For example, when God blesses you with kids, your character becomes even more exposed. Except kids don't merely reveal your selfishness; they emulate it perfectly—and mirror it back to you at all the worst times. Quite simply, there's no circumstance that will magically change your character.

GOD WON'T PROMOTE YOU BASED ON YOUR POTENTIAL CHARACTER, ONLY YOUR PRESENT CHARACTER.

Even worse, the Pot-of-Gold Myth also tempts us to procrastinate in making changes to critical areas. "As soon as I get a promotion, *then* I'll start being financially generous." "Once I get a better boss, *then* I'll work harder!" "As soon as summer comes, *then* I'll have time to read my Bible." But God won't promote you based on your *potential* character, only your *present* character.

A Christian man once told me, "If only I could meet a really good-looking Christian girl, I don't think I'd struggle with porn as much"—implying that his lust problem was merely a response to his current girlfriend's lackluster body. The father in me wanted to punch him in the face, but the pastor in me thought, *Stop. You can hire someone to do that later.*

Instead, I said, "News Flash. If you're a lusty flirt before you get married, you'll be a lusty flirt after you get married, no matter who you marry. King Solomon had a harem of the prettiest women in the world, and it didn't slow down his lust one bit. Secondly, who you are is who you attract. Don't expect a princess if you're not a prince. Besides, what kind of good heavenly Father would entrust His princess to you?"

By this point, of course, he got defensive and said, "What I do in my private life won't affect her!" Unfortunately, research says otherwise.

Here are the real porn facts:

- If you view porn, your spouse is 43 percent more likely to experience depression—being married to a porn viewer doubles your rate of depression.[46]
- If you view porn, your spouse is 22 percent more likely to also have a food addiction or eating disorder.[47]

- Women generally experience a 40 percent reduction in
  self-esteem after marrying a man who views porn.[48]

And all of these things can still happen, even if your spouse keeps it a secret!

You see, your character will always dictate your capacity to be blessed or to stay blessed. Underdeveloped character is like gold coins in a pocket filled with holes. It's not only futile to search for new coins, but you'll fail to keep the ones you have. This is why the apostle Paul begs us: "I urge you to live a life worthy of the calling you have received" (Eph. 4:1). God has already given you an amazing calling, a path of overwhelming success that will reveal Him to the world. He has a path of life that is prefilled with golden opportunities. That path might include a spouse, a family, and a host of other wonderful things. So stop worrying about opportunities! Focus, instead, on your pocket that is full of holes.

We all need to stop and absorb this fact: God is already madly in love with us and longs for us to accomplish enormous things. Why, then, do we waste time begging for opportunities and promotions? Even sillier, why do we strive and search for blessings as if God can't bring them to us (1 Sam. 2:7ff). That's wasteful living and squandered praying. Rather, focus on living a life that's capable of handling the responsibility of your calling. *Pray less for promotion. Pray more for a promotable life!*

SURVIVING THE PROMISED LAND

This promotion issue is why God was so strict with the Israelites before they entered the Promised Land. He knew wealth, abundance, and promotion wouldn't solve their character issues. Rather, the Promised Land would challenge, amplify, and expose their character issues.

That's why God required His people to "consecrate themselves" before entering the land (Josh. 3:5). Even more, God required a mass circumcision ritual (Josh. 5:2) because He wanted to make sure the Israelites were truly devoted to Him.

God knew the Promised Land was filled with grave temptations. The people in Canaan were notorious for believing that kids were nothing more than objects for sexual pleasure. Child sex-trafficking was rampant. Indeed, children were so worthless to Canaanite cultures that they often sacrificed them to their gods—which is why God was so unsympathetic about "vomiting [the Canaanites] out of the land" (Lev. 18:25, 58). God made it clear that low sexual standards always give way to victimizing kids.[49]

Let me tell you how bad this was among the Canaanites. These people had a popular idol named Molech, an intimidating bronze statue with the head of an ox and a body like a human, sitting on a throne. With outreached arms to hold sacrifices, Molech was heated by the fire until he glowed an intense red. With heavy drums to drown out the screams, people would lay their children into the scalding hands of Molech to burn alive as an act of worship.[50]

This practice sounds so repulsive that it's hard for us to imagine it being popular. Yet this Canaanite ritual was so contagious that God had to remind His people *five times* in Scripture—all the way up through King David's era—to stop doing this. In fact, one reason God divided Solomon's kingdom was that he had allowed one of his wives to rebuild an idol of Molech (1 Kings 11:5, 7, 31–33)! You see, all promotions have a dark side, and we forget that the land flowing with milk and honey is also flowing with temptations, rationalizations, and dangers.

So the meaning of the mass circumcision in Joshua 5 wasn't lost on anyone. It was meant as a stark contrast to Canaanite practices. God wanted to make it clear: *consecration precedes promotion.*

In many ways, things haven't changed. Did you know, for instance, that the world spends more money on porn in a single week than it would cost to solve poverty in Africa? The porn revenues of just China, the U.S, Japan, and South Korea alone surpass $236 million dollars *a day*.[51] In contrast, every day 21,000 children die from poverty-related illnesses—and this number only counts the kids who are five and under.[52] And yet, the world "doesn't have the money" to prevent this? Perhaps we're not all that different from the Canaanite culture after all.

Did you know that the porn industry, which makes more revenue than all professional sports combined, spends a massive amount of money trying to convince us that porn is a victimless crime— even though porn is directly connected to increased sexual discontentment, depression, rape, and violence?[53] In every country with a growing porn industry, there's an increase in rape crimes—which is why worldwide there's an unprecedented 120 million girls who have been sexually abused or raped before age twenty.[54] Around 20 percent of internet porn comes from coerced or trafficked children.[55] So how is this a victimless crime?

We might not be laying children into the arms of Molech anymore, but a person could easily make a case that the world is ripe for a new consecration moment. The need for character is more urgent than ever, and God is paying close attention to those who are ready for promotion.

My point is this: If you've ever wondered why God would target men's private parts with a circumcision ritual, the above stats might give us a clue.[56]

Still, I have to wonder, *Did God laugh when He first commanded that men be circumcised?* At the very least, I'll bet God leaned over to a nearby angel and said with a smirk, "Watch Joshua's face when I tell him this next command." I always imagine Joshua gulping nervously while listening to God: "Uh, LORD . . . um . . . would You tell this directly to the assembly for me, so they don't think I'm making this stuff up? Besides, You have a fantastic thunder voice . . . Or could You invent email and just send them a memo?" If there was ever a leadership moment that would test the extent of your influence, asking 600,000 adult men to, well, "sharpen the ol' flint rock" would be it.

Think about it. How did Joshua first broach the subject? Imagine the masses of people gathered outside the Tent of Meeting, awaiting Joshua's next orders: "Hear, O Israel! The Lord says that, uh, well, I'm not quite sure how to explain this, but . . ."

No wonder God told Joshua to "be strong and very courageous" (Josh. 1:7)! Let's not kid ourselves: Joshua wasn't suggesting laser surgery with anesthesia. More likely, this was your great uncle Abinadab (the one with the steady hand) behind the tent. I mean, there are a thousand ways this could go wrong. And, undoubtedly, this inspired many people to pray.

But there's a simple lesson here: *We don't want our Promised Lands unless we're ready. We don't want promotion unless we're promotable.* God's tests of consecration may seem extreme, but the costs of unfaithful living are far more extreme—perhaps even eternal.

I'm not saying that every delay in our dreams is due to a hidden sin or impurity. Sometimes our hearts are fully devoted, but our skills aren't fully developed. Even then, remember: Your soul finds rest in God alone (Ps. 62:1). There will never be a spouse, a job, an income level, or an opportunity that fills the God-shaped void in your life.

So the next time you feel left behind or left out, don't rant that "the world can't see your talent." Don't whine about leaders who "don't deserve it." As the Scriptures say about Joseph: Until the time came to fulfill Joseph's dreams, the Lord tested Joseph's character (Ps. 105:19). Your time is coming, too, so don't make the fatal mistake of focusing on all the wrong things.

PROCLAIM

Father, I acknowledge that You alone know when I'm ready for promotion. You see my future obstacles, temptations, and stressors that I can't see. So rather than looking for dream opportunities, I choose to focus on dream character. Help me to "live a life worthy of the calling" that I have already received. Amen.

KEY IDEAS

1. The world is constantly trying to sell us solutions that don't solve our problems.

2. Sales psychologists regularly exploit us to make decisions that aren't necessarily logical.

3. When we romanticize or demonize the future, we tend to obsess over the things that confirm our biases, while leaving out other details. This can result in devastating mistakes.

4. Many of us are deceived by the Talent Myth, which is the idea that "an exceedingly developed talent is the primary ingredient that qualifies me for promotion—more than character, experience, perseverance, loyalty, or leadership."

5. God loves us too much to promote us without thoroughly testing our character, perseverance, and capacity to handle such an opportunity.

6. Many of us are deceived by the Pot-of-Gold Myth: the idea that some golden opportunity, promotion, or person, will improve our character. But promotion never improves our character; rather it magnifies and reveals it.

7. God has already given you a great calling, a path of overwhelming success that will reveal Him to the world. You don't need to worry about that. Instead, focus on "living a life worthy of the calling we have received" (Eph. 4:1).

8. When we seek promotions God isn't giving us, we just fail bigger, and we condemn ourselves to an eternal search for better circumstances rather than living a lifestyle worthy of better circumstances.

9. All promotions have a dark side. We forget that the land flowing with milk and honey is also flowing with temptations and dangers. This is why God required consecration before letting His people enter it.

10. God won't promote you based on your potential character, only your present character.

DISCUSSION QUESTIONS

1. Do you think advertising and marketing can have an effect on our happiness? Or do you think we're growing immune to the thousands of messages we see every day?

2. Have you ever made a decision that didn't turn out as you expected? Do you think any of the above-mentioned brain-hacks had anything to do with it? (E.g., the bandwagon impulse—an obsessive impulse to prefer things with momentum, even if they aren't better; or the confirmation bias impulse—an obsession with details that confirms our already-existing preferences; or the too-many-options-creates-procrastination flaw.)

3. How do you know if your decisions are being influenced by your own "confirmation bias"? How might a person keep from being self-deceived while making a decision?

4. What's the "elusive circumstance" that you're most inclined to pray for right now (the promotion, goal, or pot-of-gold circumstances you're most inclined to obsess over)?

5. Have you ever felt tempted to take dangerous shortcuts toward the circumstance you had in mind in question 4? If so, explain. If not, could there be any dangerous shortcuts you haven't yet identified in your circumstance?

6. If the Devil were to sabotage your character (to mess up your promotability), what specific area would he target: finances, sexuality, contentment, lack of Sabbath, weight and overeating, marriage or dating?

7. Did any of the pornography stats stick out to you? Is there such a thing as a "victimless sin"?

8. Can you think of any examples in which people's talent clearly exceeded their character? If so, name some. How do you think the circumstances might have undermined the happiness of the people involved?

9. Do you feel like "God is for you and that He has a great calling on your life"? Why or why not? How do you think this feeling affects you or your prayer life?

10. What are some of the benefits of focusing on our character rather than our circumstances?

THE GREAT
HOT DOG SNATCHER

*What If God Intentionally Allows Irritating People in Our Lives to Help
Us Realize Only He Can Affect Our Promotions?*

P eople ask me why I pray so much. They're hoping I'll share
some super-spiritual pearl of wisdom. But the main reason
I pray is that prayer keeps me from wanting to kill people.
I often tell pastors if you can survive ten years of pastoring without
committing murder, you'll do well in this vocation. And if you mess
this up, God always needs more people for prison ministry.

Strangely enough, research shows that "clergy" rank as the eighth
most likely profession for psychopaths![57] I'm not kidding. That is a
legit research fact! Remember, psychopaths can be charming individuals. So it raises the question: How do you know if your pastor
is one of them? Here are three possible indicators:

1. DOES HE OR SHE HOLD PEOPLE UNDERWATER EXTRA LONG
DURING BAPTISMS?

He may say it's because "immersion baptism is more biblical

than sprinkling," but there might be a naughty little motive lurking there.

2. DOES HE OR SHE PUNCH PEOPLE WHO DON'T GIVE MONEY TO THE CHURCH?

Quite often, nongiving church attendees will complain that the church isn't doing enough [fill-in-the-blank]. And you, as the pastor, should change this (not realizing that the problem they're complaining about would immediately be solved if they gave consistently). When these opinionated moochers vent at me, I mentally punch them. However, if your pastor actually does this, he or she may be a psychopath.

3. DOES HE OR SHE MAKE CHILDREN REENACT DAVID AND GOLIATH WITH REAL WEAPONS?

"But, it makes the Bible more memorable!" he or she might argue. Keep your ears tuned. *Silence of the Lambs* may sound like a catchy Passover sermon series, but don't be fooled.

In all fairness, clinical psychopaths aren't necessarily violent. They simply don't integrate emotions like most people do, so it's not a surprise that they tend to thrive in vocations that experience enormous amounts of critique and pressure.[58] There are times when I wish I had the ability to turn off my emotions.

But how do "normal" people deal with difficult individuals? When I ask people "what do you think is the biggest obstacle to your dreams?" quite often, their obstruction isn't a what but a who. "If only my spouse / family / boss / leader would [fill-in-the-blank], *then* I'd be closer to my dreams."

I can empathize with this feeling. Over the years, a lot of people have let me down, but one of my most memorable betrayals was the "Great Hot Dog Snatcher of 1999." As a young senior pastor, I was a bit naïve. At that time I still believed that everyone is reasonable.

I made silly statements like, "Deep down, all people want to do the right thing." But all of my idealism was shattered one terrible Sunday in 1999.

At around five o'clock one Sunday morning, I got a phone call from the police about a church crisis. I can't explain the details, but suffice it to say, you generally don't want the police to give you your wake-up call. Actually, you *never* want them to be the ones who wake you up.

Now, before you try to imagine what would merit such a call, don't worry. The traumatic event isn't the critical part of this story. Rather, it's merely the backdrop to what happened later that day.

After a flurry of traumatic meetings and church services, I had to hurry off to even more distressing meetings all afternoon. I didn't eat anything all morning, and so I was starving. I was afraid that if I didn't grab some kind of food on the way to my next emergency meeting, I probably wouldn't be able to eat all day.

Unfortunately, there were no fast food restaurants nearby. The only food option available was a truck stop gas station. Inside, it looked as though every trucker in the county had ravaged every last Hot Pocket and microwavable egg burrito. All that remained was the ancient hot dog warmer faithfully rotating in the corner. It was my last option, so I made a beeline to the bin of crusty buns.

Now if you're going to have gas station dogs ("petro-wienies," as I like to call them), you've got to drown out the plastic "meat flavor" by using every condiment at your disposal (ketchup, relish, mustard, mayo, etc). So there I was, prepping my buns when some-one came up behind me. I turned around to see a pleasant-looking, middle-aged woman waiting for her chance at the hot dog warmer. Knowing that I'm rather slow, I pointed to my artfully arranged hot dog buns and told her, "You can go ahead! I'm kind of picky when it comes to the application of my relish" (or something similar that sounded less nerdy).

After letting her go in front of me, I continued to color each bun with precision stripes of ketchup. But as I stood there . . . she went and took every last hot dog off the warmer! There had been something like fifteen hotdogs! She even took the over-cooked polish sausage!

Out of the goodness of my heart, I had allowed her to go ahead of me—and I was betrayed! But how do you confront someone for *that*? "Hey, you! You took my hot dog!" Or "You! You're a wiener snatcher!"

There are a million ways this confrontation can go wrong, and as I frantically searched for the right words, she hit the register. Before I could assemble a strategy to recapture one or two dogs, she was gone—a thief in the night! As I stood there, stunned, all I could hear was the moaning of an empty hot dog warmer, slowly rotating behind me.

Now some of you are thinking, *What's the big deal? It's just a hot-dog or two or fifteen.*" But it's the principle of the matter! I lived by a code of hot dog chivalry, and I got cooked.

After years of counseling, I'm trying to assume the best of that woman. Perhaps she was a poor single mom, looking out for an entire household of starving British orphans. I could hear them weeping, "Please Mum! Might we have one last frankfurter before we die?" Perhaps the guilt over her crime even caused her to sob all the way home as she imagined me standing alone and hungry. My point is this: If you log a few years on planet earth, you'll experience self-centered, thoughtless people. Rejection and hurt are a certainty.

NO PERSON OR INSTITUTION CAN ULTIMATELY OBSTRUCT GOD'S BLESSINGS FOR YOU!

So who is the source of your pain? Whose failures are you most inclined to rehearse? A coworker, family member, politician, institution? Who do you find yourself debating with in your head? Who do you feel betrayed by? Don't feel bad if you have a couple of them—or a stadium full. The earth is filled with cold-blooded wiener snatchers.

It's easy to feel like people obstruct our dreams, but I have amazing news for you: No person or institution can ultimately obstruct God's blessings for you! In fact, no human can prevent you from experiencing God's promotion, except *you*. Or, as Hebrews 13:6 puts it, "The Lord is my helper; I will not be afraid. What can mere mortals do to me?" Truth is, no matter what people do with the intention of harming us, God can intend that same thing for good (Gen. 50:20). And this leads to our next myth:

MYTH

THE GOLIATH MYTH:
People can stand in the way of my happiness or God's promotion.

Obviously, the Goliath Myth comes from the classic story of David and Goliath in 1 Samuel 17. But this classic duel is a bazillion times more profound when you interpret it in light of the previous seventeen chapters of 1 Samuel.

First Samuel starts by recounting a variety of leaders and how they interacted with the presence of God. In story after story, God makes it clear that *He is the only One who promotes and demotes* (1 Sam. 2:6–9). No adversary can stand in the way of our promotion—unless we sabotage ourselves with our own ill character by fearing people more than God (1 Sam. 2:3, 10).

Unfortunately, in the first seventeen chapters of 1 Samuel, we see more bad examples than good—which is what makes David so refreshing. When David killed Goliath, David wasn't the king yet. At the time, God's kingdom was entrusted to Saul. It's easy to forget that Saul could have been the one to kill Goliath, but he flunked the test. Why? Because he believed that people—specifically, a tall person named Goliath—could stand in the way of God's promotion.

When David insisted on facing Goliath, there's an awkward part of the story where Saul insisted that David use his armor (1 Sam. 17:38), which certainly seems to imply that Saul should have been the one to face Goliath in the first place. Saul over-inflated another man's power, and that's one of the reasons God found him unfit to be king (1 Sam. 15:24).

THREE SIDE EFFECTS OF BELIEVING THE GOLIATH MYTH

If you're like me, when you read this story, you like to imagine that you'd be David, boldly taking on insurmountable odds with the power of God. But quite often, we're a lot more like Saul. We believe the Goliath Myth.

So how does one know if they're buying the myth? There are three specific symptoms to look for.

1. REHASHING HUMAN FAILURES

If you rehearse people's sins more than God's power over sin, it's a sign you don't understand God's power.

One time I was hurt by a coworker, and for a season, all I wanted to do was grumble about this person. My grumbling eventually spilled over into my prayer life.

Have you ever "prayer-grumbled"? It happens when you merge praying with worrying and whining—a.k.a., whimper-intercession.

So I started whimper-ceding: *God, I can't believe this person was so self-centered and thoughtless.* My brain went off on all of the inconveniences this person had caused me.

Abruptly, I sensed the Holy Spirit impress upon my heart: *Peter, do you trust Me to take care of this situation? Do you trust Me to bring about justice and restitution as it pertains to this person?*

After a brief pause, I acquiesced: *Yes, Lord, I trust You.*

Then, why do you keep bringing this up? echoed into my heart.

Rehashing people's failures is a sign of two things: (1) that we haven't effectively forgiven them yet,[59] and (2) we're not convinced God's power is greater than this individual.

As I pointed out in chapter 3, our prayers often reveal our pathologies. And here's another application of this: You know you're dying spiritually when you rehearse people's sins more than God's power over sin.

When you get hurt it's easy to become obsessed with other people's power more than God's power. But remember, loved ones, God doesn't like to take a backseat to anything, so He is certain to test us on this point. God will gladly allow all sorts of irritating people to enter our lives until we stop believing the Goliath Myth. So the real question is this: How many betrayals, rejections, and letdowns will it take before you learn to trust your heavenly Father?

2. OVERINFLATING THE POWER OF THOSE AROUND YOU

If you think back to chapter 2, I talked a lot about humanity's illusion of control. We love to believe we control more than we actually do. And we love to believe that *other people* have more control than they actually do.

Like I shared in chapter 3, I knew my boss had control over a way larger budget than I did, and whenever I felt overwhelmed or overworked, I was quick to think about this fact. However, he also had fifty times the number of people begging him for his budget and then critiquing him for how he spent it; thus he actually had *less* freedom and control than I did. But at that time, I was perfectly comfortable with overinflating his actual power in my mind—until I got his job and *I* was completely overwhelmed.

Many people also like to believe that politicians have unlimited resources to change things. Are you kidding? When you spend half your workday shaking hands and kissing babies, there's not a whole lot of time left to change the world.

Whenever our dreams and expectations exceed our resources, we become overwhelmed. In these times, it's easy to overinflate the resources and capabilities of people above us, beside us, and below us. To make this worse, social media tends to reinforce the illusion. Everyone on social media looks like they're always partying, falling in love, and going on vacation, while we sit at home watching television with our pet gerbils.

Sure, it might *feel* like everyone's got it easier, but let me assure you, we look at people's filtered high points and then contrast them with our lows. People rarely have as much time, money, happiness, or control as we like to think they do.

3. PLAYING THE "VICTIM CARD"

At some point or another, all of us will experience discrimination because of age, ethnicity, gender, faith, and so-forth. Over the years, you are destined to run into a few selfish and insecure people who will use their influence to hurt you. When these things happen, it's easy to play the "victim card," which is just another way of saying, "God, this person is more powerful than You."

Don't misunderstand me. Discrimination is real, and we need to fight

DAVID BELIEVED THAT THE MORE PEOPLE CAN AVOID PLAYING THE VICTIM EVEN WHEN THEY ARE THE VICTIM, THE MORE IT WILL ENABLE GOD TO ACT ON THEIR BEHALF.

injustice wherever we find it. We forget that the Philistine story of Goliath is an account of racial tension. The Philistines had a technological monopoly on iron—which they used systematically to oppress other people groups (1 Sam. 13:19). But David believed that the more people can avoid playing the victim even when they are the victim, the more it will enable God to act on their behalf. *Playing the victim is one of the most fundamental ways to strip ourselves of divine power.*[60] As a result, David was promotable while Saul was not.

Of course, the reason we play the victim card is twofold: (1) We use it to evoke compassion from people, and (2) it deflects attention away from our performance and character. The problem with this strategy, however, is that it's impossible to play a victim and be a victor at the same time. To play the victim we have to point the finger to achieve these results, which only angers people around us and pulls our focus away from the primary thing we can change: *ourselves.* Even worse, we can't antagonize people and influence them at the same time. Thus, when we use victimization to draw people to our causes, we simultaneously undermine our ability to influence our adversaries—which is why God calls us to "bless those who persecute [us]" (Rom. 12:14).

Even more, when we hang out with people who play the victim card, it will statistically increase our odds of depression![61] Ouch! Quite simply, the Goliath myth is a virus.

Once again, there will always be a "Goliath" or a "Philistine oppression" to fight. But as we fight these injustices, we've got to avoid the victim mentality that often accompanies such battles. You plus God always equals a majority. There's no earthly system or evil industry that can continually obstruct your promotion—as long as you've got the faith and character to honor this divine partnership.

Notice I used the phrase "continually obstruct." People can still do hurtful things. Sometimes, it feels like God doesn't see our oppression—which is why one of the theme verses of 1 Samuel says, "The Lord is a God who knows, and by him deeds are weighed" (1 Sam. 2:3).

If you think God doesn't see or hear your struggles, you're wrong.[62] He's working His plan, and sometimes that plan takes time.

In David's story, for example, God told David he was going to be king (1 Sam. 16). Suddenly, David got promoted from sheep herding to harp playing for King Saul! This was like going from total loser to being the headline band on a major rock tour (1 Sam 16:19). Then, one chapter later, David slayed Goliath. It seemed like David had nowhere to go but up! You would think his life would suddenly become blissful. Yet the next nineteen chapters or so recount a decade of complete and total torture for David.

This wasn't merely ten years of inconvenience; it was repeated murder attempts, multiple escapes, and constant betrayals. There must have been a moment when David shouted, "God! What kind of promotion is this?"

BEING ANOINTED DOESN'T MAKE YOU READY

Keep in mind, David was merely *anointed* as king. This didn't mean he was the king. Many people falsely assume that their anointing (gifts, skills, and talents) automatically qualifies them for a position of authority, but healthy promotion always requires testing.

Remember the Talent Myth? It's the faulty belief that "an exceedingly developed talent is the primary ingredient that qualifies me for promotion—more than character, experience, perseverance, loyalty, or leadership." Like I said, God loves us too much to curse us with opportunity. He always tests us first, and quite often, the greater the anointing, the greater the testing.

Recently, a study found that "40 percent of America's Millennials, (those born between 1977–1997) believe they should be promoted every two years regardless of their performance."[63] In fact, the rate of clinical narcissism in Millennials is more than three times higher than previous generations.[64] But how does this sabotage our happiness?

In case you don't read nerdy psychology books, narcissism is a measurement of several attributes: your patience in earning promotions, your openness to critique, your ability to imagine your actions through other people's viewpoints, and your likelihood to base your decisions on self-interest. (If you're curious, you can take free tests online that will reveal your degree of narcissism!)[65]

Not surprisingly, these tendencies have caused young people to change jobs with unprecedented frequency. As a result, many HR departments now ignore resumes coming from people who stay at jobs less than three to five years.[66] Why? Because in certain vocations, it can cost companies a lot of money to train a person. In many cases, an employee doesn't really add much benefit to an organization until that person has been there a few years.[67]

Economists are starting to make the case that *loyal* people statistically make far more money than *talented* people.[68] And this shouldn't surprise us. It's actually a biblical principle.[69]

One thing is for sure: If we think our bosses, coworkers or "the system" is holding us back from promotion, then we certainly aren't ready for promotion! Why? Because we're fixated on all the wrong things. The Bible tells us: "No one from the east or the west . . . can exalt themselves. It is God who judges: He brings one down, he exalts another" (Ps. 75:6–7).

Yes, the world around us may be racist, sexist, and determined to make us fail, but according to Scripture, they are nothing! God "sits enthroned above the circle of the earth, and its people are like grasshoppers. . . . He brings princes to naught and reduces the rulers of this world to nothing" (Isa. 40:22–23).

You can object, "But I'm being chased by a giant grasshopper!" You can rant about your problem always being "out there," but remember: "The LORD sends poverty and wealth; he humbles and he exalts" (1 Sam. 2:7).

So here is the question you *should* focus on: If God is loving and powerful and yet isn't sending me promotion, then why? If God "sends wealth" and you've got none . . . why might that be? You can blame the Devil. You can blame the person being used by the Devil. You can blame God (as if He's either not loving or not powerful). But what if something deeper is occurring? What if God is patiently using pain to remove our sinful natures—to undermine the myths we believe? What if God is preparing us for the ultimate promotion?

THE GREATER THE ANOINTING, THE GREATER THE TESTING

Ironically, Goliath was one of the "smallest" adversaries David had to face. After killing Goliath, David experienced far worse. Even more ironic, the only human who ever truly impeded David's promotion was himself (2 Sam. 12:7–9). And the same holds true for you and me when it comes to promotion and happiness.

Why does God test us? Because He loves us, and the greater the anointing, the greater the testing.

There were so many low moments for David in 1 Samuel that it's hard to believe so many bad things could happen to one man. Including the decade I mentioned earlier, he faced close to seventeen years' worth of low moments. His boss, King Saul, tried to kill him over and over. (And you thought you had a bad boss.) Then David fled to Naioth at Ramah (1 Sam. 19). He had to hide in a field for several days to avoid a death squad. Finally, he had to flee to Gath, yet he almost got killed there, too! After that, he fled, again, to the Cave of Adullam (1 Sam. 22:1); then to Moab (v. 3); then to Judah (v. 5); then to Keilah (1 Sam. 23:2); then to the Desert of Ziph (where he was betrayed by the Ziphites); then to the Desert of Maon (1 Sam. 23:25); then to the strongholds of En Gedi (v. 29); then *back* to Maon; and *back* to Ziph, where he was betrayed *again* (1 Sam. 26:1).

These are just random cities to you and me, but to David, each of these moves was devastating! Each change required him to start over. Most of them likely created post-traumatic stress. With every move, he had to reset his dreams.

Perhaps you've lost a job, marriage, or family member. These can be devastating changes, to be sure. So imagine wave after wave of losses for over a decade.

As if it couldn't get any worse, David had to consider the unthinkable: go to the land of the Philistines. Remember, David was the equivalent of Osama Bin Laden to the Philistines. He had killed their hero Goliath. Yet in desperation, he went there (27:1), and after painstakingly proving he wasn't a threat to them, he got attacked anyway.

I suppose David could console himself with the fact that, despite having to constantly move, his own men were loyal to him. However, after his village was attacked in Gath, even his own men talked about stoning him (1 Sam. 30)! The very people he had *helped the most* wanted to kill him. How much worse could it get?

A *lot* worse! In fact, all this happened right around the same time his city was torched (with all of his possessions), and his family was kidnapped. But in the midst of all this pain, 1 Samuel 30:6 says, "David found strength in the LORD his God." What? I almost lost my salvation over a hot dog snatcher, and yet David seems unflappable! Clearly, he had a resilience that most of us do not.

So the million dollar question is this: *How did David stay so close to God when so many bad things were happening?* Over the years, I've been captivated by the question: What made David so resilient? And why do the rest of us look like such wimps by comparison?

In the next chapter, I'm going to highlight two specific betrayals that reveal David's radically different way of thinking. If you seriously study the life of David, you will notice that he repeatedly made decisions that are downright counterintuitive. We'll look at two stories that have perplexed people for centuries, and out of them, we're going to explore five theological convictions that gave David a jaw-dropping promotability.

So, the question becomes "Do you have them?"

You'll soon find out.

PROCLAIM

Lord, there is no human being or earthly system that can hold back the power of Your promotion in my life. Therefore, I will not compromise my character or allow anyone to steal the joy that can only come from You.

KEY IDEAS

1. No human being can ultimately obstruct our promotion except ourselves.

2. God routinely allows promotion to pass by people who believe the Goliath Myth.

3. We all have a tendency to imagine that people have more power than God.

4. God is so passionate about exposing this lie that He will even allow irritating people into our lives until we change.

5. Unforgiveness and rehearsing people's failures is a clear sign that we believe people have more power than God.

6. We all tend to believe that everyone around us has more power, resources, and culpability than they actually have. This overinflation of other people's power is a secondary symptom of believing the Goliath Myth.

7. We all tend to play the "victim card" to evoke compassion from people and to deflect attention away from our issues—not realizing that this strips us of divine power.

8. We often assume (wrongly) that talent and skill alone qualify us for promotion and that testing shouldn't play a significant role.

9. We often fail to understand that the greater the promotion, the more necessary the testing.

10. A deeper study of David's unique theology is critical if we want to have a similar promotability.

DISCUSSION QUESTIONS

1. Have you ever been betrayed or wounded by someone? How did it make you feel?

2. Why do you think "rehearsing people's failures" is a sign of unforgiveness?

3. Is it possible to forgive someone in a single moment?

4. Have you ever "inflated someone's power"—seen someone as having all of the resources and solutions—and then changed your mind later?

5. Why do you think it's easier to blame others than to look at our own issues?

6. What are some practical ways people play the victim card and how can you stop doing that?

7. Why do you think the victim card grieves God? What does playing it say about Him?

8. Have you ever given up on a job, task, or person prematurely? What do you think contributed to such a decision?

9. Why would a "greater calling" or promotion require a greater level of testing?

10. Why do you think people throughout the centuries have been fascinated with David?

6

THE FIVE PILLARS OF PROMOTION

Lessons from One of the Most Promoted People in History

L ike many leaders, I've had to endure a good amount of false accusations. One of the worst came from a blogger after I wrote my book *Pharisectomy*. I knew some people would have a hard time reading a book that mixes comedy and spiritual growth, but one guy got his feathers so ruffled that he devoted an entire podcast to "the cult leader, Peter Haas." There are some days when I *wish* I was a cult leader. Perhaps then, at least a few people would finally listen to me.

One of my cult mandates would be that we never hold hands when we pray. Yes, I'm a bit germaphobic. But even more, there's always somebody on one side who has sweaty palms and squeezes like they're in a test of strength. On the other side is the person who holds their hand really high, so I end up holding their entire arm in the air as if it's a dumbbell at the gym. As the prayer rambles on, I desperately want to relax my trembling shoulder muscle, but any and all movements feel like I'm disturbing the Holy Spirit. So if I were a cult leader, I would at least mandate that everyone wear soft fuzzy gloves while hanging their hands super low.

Let's go back to the mean-spirited blogger. The main problem was that he podcasted all kinds of false assertions about what I believe. And soon enough, people started quoting his misquotes. The next thing you know, our church started getting phone calls from Christians all around, freaking out: "I heard that Pastor Peter believes in [fill-in-the-heresy]! Why would he say that?" It was crazy stuff—things I would *never* say.

As the problem snowballed, I started feeling victimized. After all, this podcast preacher was nothing more than a schoolyard bully. Scripture says that "wisdom from heaven" is "peace-loving, considerate, submissive, full of mercy" (James 3:17), so if the preachers you listen to lack a "submissive" or "mercy-filled tone," their wisdom is not from heaven. But the attacks continued. It seemed like every week, this self-appointed defender of truth would take his bullying to new levels. I actually looked into filing a defamation lawsuit against him—a path that was tremendously expensive, to say nothing of being biblically questionable.

Throughout the period of bullying, I felt powerless. "*God*, I wondered, *how can you let such twisted people go unpunished? Why does justice seem to take so long?*

People are so cynical about pastors in general that the moment someone accuses me of something, many people assume it to be true. But the only reason it affected me was because a large part of me still believed the Goliath Myth. I still believed people could continually stand in the way of both my happiness and God's promotion. I felt like God wasn't defending me, which wasn't true at all. In reality, God was drawing me to Himself.

As I explained in the last chapter, God is so passionate about exposing the Goliath Myth in our lives that He will allow irritating people into our lives until we learn that His power is greater. All of us will eventually ask, "Why did this person hurt me?" or "Why does it seem like this person is getting away with these things?" Often, the fact that we're even asking these questions is a sign that we're missing the whole point. This type of thinking, by itself, is a symptom of a greater disease God is determined to fight.

So listen to me, loved ones, no one can ultimately stand in the way of your promotion (Heb. 13:6)! The Bible says, "All people are like grass" (Isa.40:6). God simply breathes and "the grass withers and the flowers fall" (v. 7). And in Isaiah 40:15: "the nations are like a drop in a bucket." Therefore,

> Why do you complain, Jacob? Why do you say, Israel, "My way is hidden from the Lord; my cause is disregarded by my God?" Do you not know? Have you not heard? The Lord is the everlasting God, the Creator of the ends of the earth. He will not grow tired or weary. (Isa. 40:27–28)

Perhaps, as you read this, it might feel like someone is standing in the way of your promotion or happiness. Frankly, that person isn't your problem. Your problem is that you fundamentally don't believe your heavenly Father will take care of you. Hopefully, by the end of this chapter you'll master several new tools to cut out these cancerous thoughts.

You'll remember that David seemed to have a million enemies: Goliath, Saul, Achish, Doeg, Nabal, Hadadezer, Joab, Ish-Bosheth, Hanun, Absalom, Shimei, Ahithophel, Sheba, Adonijah and Abiathar. And those were just the ringleaders! Every one of these names represents serious pain. They equaled sleepless months, raped family members, murdered friends, kidnapped kids, and broken hearts. You'd think David would be one of the most bitter, controlling, vindictive people around, and yet, listen to what he wrote: "Cast your cares on the LORD and he will sustain you; he will never let the righteous be shaken" (Ps. 55:22).

Even more astounding, many of David's biggest problems were incited by the insecurity of a single man, King Saul. If you had asked any of David's friends, "What's David's biggest problem?" they would unanimously have agreed: King Saul. Yet, in mind-blowing contrast, David never saw Saul as his chief hindrance to being king. David saw himself hindered by his own character.

Over the next few pages, I'm going to highlight two specific betrayals that reveal the radically different way David thought about his promotions from the way we usually think. I'm going to pull out those five theological convictions I promised that gave David jaw-dropping promotability.

WHICH TO KILL: SAUL OR MY CHARACTER?

In the classic story in 1 Samuel 24, King Saul and his elite army of three thousand men were pursuing David. Saul stopped at a cave to use the bathroom, and it happened to be the very cave where David was hiding. David and several of his men crept up behind Saul, and at that moment, I imagine David's men thought, *This is amazing! This is finally where Saul's wicked reign will end! David finally gets justice. In a few days, David will become king, and we'll all live in the palace!*

But what did David do? He secretly cut off the corner of Saul's robe and spared the king's life (1 Sam. 24:4). What! Why would David spare the man who was ruthlessly trying to murder him? Because he believed that justice and promotion belong to God (1 Sam. 24:5).

David believed that rebellion, dissentious words, and dishonoring actions should never be acceptable means for achieving his goals

(Exod. 22:28). Part of this was because, someday soon, he knew God would make *him* king, and he didn't want to reap what he sowed (Gal. 6:7).

Even more stunning, David's conscience was so sensitive that he was grief-stricken over the miniscule sin of wrecking Saul's robe! After Saul left the cave, David rebuked his men for even considering an attack on Saul (1 Sam. 24:7), and then David revealed himself to Saul's death squad, putting his own life at risk in order to do it.

Before we find out what happened to David, let's quickly talk about the significance of cutting off the corner of Saul's robe. David wasn't merely securing evidence to prove he had spared Saul's life. His initial goal was to humiliate Saul.

In those days, the corner of a robe had two purposes:

1. Many men hung their seal, their signature mark, on their robe. To lose it would be the ancient equivalent of losing your keys, your security badge, or your signature. The corner of your robe signified your authority.

2. The other purpose of a tassel was to remind people to obey God (see Num. 15:38-41; Deut. 22:12). If you didn't have a tassel, then you weren't in compliance with the Torah (the Bible, as they had it then). So, to cut off the tassel was to morally embarrass Saul and to cut off the very thing that would remind him to obey God. David realized that his act would actually make it harder for Saul to experience God.

David was so sensitive about maintaining his character that he would rather risk his own life than hide his small sins. And this leads us to the first of David's five unique theological convictions (UTCs).

UTC 1: DAVID OBSESSED OVER HIS OWN CHARACTER ISSUES, NOT THE ISSUES OF OTHERS.

Of all times to suddenly grow a conscience, this was the worst time, but David was concerned about only one thing: his character before God. He knew that if he took care of his promotability, God would take care of his promotion.

David's actions seem foreign to those of us who are accustomed to taking matters into our own hands. Like I shared in the last chapter, some of us love to play the victim card. As long as the problem is "out there," it takes the pressure and focus off of us. But God isn't fooled by such tactics. David knew that God had to flunk Saul because of character issues. So if David overlooked his own sin, what made him any different than Saul?

After cutting off Saul's tassel, David did the unthinkable. He shouted out to Saul and his army of three thousand! You can imagine David's men were probably hiding nearby, completely astonished at their leader's actions. It must have seemed like David was initiating a suicide mission. To be specific, David feared God three thousand times more than he feared men. And remember, this bold move was coming from the same man who took on Goliath.

BOTH PROMOTION AND AUTHORITY COME FROM GOD ALONE, AND ULTIMATELY, BOTH PROMOTION AND AUTHORITY CAN BE LOST IF GOD CEASES TO BE NUMBER ONE IN OUR LIVES.

David shouted, "May the LORD judge between you and me. And may the Lord avenge the wrongs you have done to me, but my hand will not touch you" (1 Sam. 24:12). I'm sure that everyone stood there in stunned silence, waiting for Saul to respond.

Under the conviction of the Holy Spirit, King Saul started weeping, "May the LORD reward you well for the way you treated me today. I know that you will surely be king and that the kingdom of Israel will be established in your hands" (1 Sam. 24:19–20). Can you imagine seeing this? No matter which side you were on, it was a mind-boggling moment.

UTC 2: DAVID LEFT VENGEANCE TO GOD.

David was so confident in God's promotion that he was willing to face a bloodthirsty Saul and his army of elite soldiers. In the end, David knew that no one—not even a king—can remain standing in the way of God's promotion (Isa. 40:23) or God's vengeance. Both promotion and authority come from God alone, and ultimately, both promotion and authority can be lost if God ceases to be number one in our lives.

Sadly, a bit later David lost his authority for a brief season. Thankfully, as we will soon see, David was quick to repent. So allow me to expand on this context for our second betrayal story: David vs. Shimei.

SHIMEI TO THE LEFT

You may notice that Shimei is not a particularly intimidating sounding name. "Goliath," on the other hand, has an extra shovel full of manliness to it. But Shimei? It sounds more like a dance move—the Shimei Shake—than a tough guy. But David's confrontation with Shimei reveals a few more of David's distinct convictions.

To give the story a bit of context, one chapter earlier—in 2 Samuel 15—we read about the rebellion of Absalom, one of David's sons. After nursing along some bitterness for years, Absolom finally staged a coup that ended up killing tens of thousands of people. He ran King David out of town, and then Absalom began raping his father's wives in public. Once again, the now former King David was running barefoot into a foreign land to save his life.

Some people would argue that David deserved part of this. After all, God promised there would be consequences for David's moral failure with Bathsheba (2 Sam. 11). Specifically, God said a rebellion would arise out of David's own household (2 Sam. 12:11). The lesson is that God holds *everyone* accountable for sin, even David. Thankfully, David was quick to publically repent of his sin with Bathsheba (v. 13),[70] but years later, as this prophetic nightmare came true, an even worse thing happened to David as he was escaping Jerusalem.

While David and his men were running, a man named Shimei started whipping rocks at them. You see, Shimei was from the clan of the former king, Saul, and he was still bitter that David had replaced Saul. So as Shimei whipped rocks at their heads, he shouted, "The LORD has repaid you for all the blood you shed in the household of Saul" (2 Sam. 16:8). It was a completely false accusation, by the way. To the contrary, David had been utterly generous toward Saul's household (2 Sam. 9:1)—a kindness that was continually snubbed by Saul's family (2 Sam. 16:3). Shimei was clearly accustomed to playing the victim.

Now, I don't know about you, but if I were having an especially bad day—like losing my entire kingdom—the last thing I would tolerate would be a guy throwing rocks at me, shouting falsehoods. If there were ever a time when I might actually be tempted to do something crazy violent, this would be it.

Apparently, David's men felt the same way. One of his warriors asked, "Why should this dead dog curse my lord the king? Let me go over and cut off his head" (2 Sam. 16:9).

To me that would have sounded like a good idea: "Why yes! Thank you my dear Abishai . . . and bring me back a Starbucks coffee, too."

But check out the shocking response David gave instead: "If he is cursing because the LORD said to him, 'Curse David,' who can ask,

'Why do you do this'" (v. 10)? In other words, David was asking: "What if I deserve this? What if God is using him to bring about a necessary repentance?" Wow! This leads us to David's third unique theological conviction.

UTC 3: DAVID REGULARLY CONSIDERED THE POSSIBILITY THAT HE MIGHT BE WRONG.

I realize this sounds more like common sense than a "unique conviction," but unfortunately, humility is a rare trait. I know hundreds of Christians who've gotten hurt by people who can't even consider the possibility that just maybe they also played a small role in the problem. We refuse to consider it because when our pain tolerance is low, so is our teachability.

We all like to imagine that we're humble or teachable, but here's a question for you: How quick are you to apologize? Do you wait for others to apologize first?

I often tell my kids: "If you're even 10 percent wrong, apologize and own it as if you're 100 percent wrong." Why? Because humility is a muscle you have to practice flexing, and only foolish people resist stretching it.

As my friend Matt Keller says, "Teachability is the ability to relearn that which you already know."[71] Or to put it another way: Teachability is the ability to endure constructive humiliation.

Let's admit it. It's hard to admit when we've screwed up. I've worked with a lot of leaders who couldn't apologize or handle constructive humiliation. I've watched pastors pinball from job to job, only to realize that constructive humiliation is the only true way up! "God opposes the proud but shows favor to the humble" (1 Peter 5:5).

Yet the good news is this: The more you believe that God is in control of your promotions, the easier it is to remain teachable.

THE MORE YOU BELIEVE THAT GOD IS IN CONTROL OF YOUR PROMOTIONS, THE EASIER IT IS TO REMAIN TEACHABLE.

If the person who's lecturing you is wrong, guess who will work it out for you? Your heavenly Father!

You may remember that before planting my current church I took over a fairly sizable regional church in Wisconsin. As a young senior pastor, I had to endure constant lectures on "what a good church looks like" from people who thought I was too young to be their pastor. Thankfully, God gave me the grace to remain life-giving through a lot of misguided rebukes.

You see, there are benefits to staying life-giving:

A. You just might learn something.

B. When God proves you right (assuming you are), you get the pleasure of leading your adversary back to wisdom. It's incredible.

If we do *our* job—which is to remain teachable—God will do *His* job, which is to promote us and justify us at the perfect time, no matter what any man or woman tries to do to us.

So, back to Shimei. David's response was the equivalent of saying, "What if God is ultimately behind this? What if God is using this to improve me?"

David continued, "Leave [Shimei] alone. . . . It may be that the LORD will look upon my misery and restore to me his covenant blessing instead of his curse today" (2 Sam 16:11–12). In other words, if it's not of the Lord, then God will take care of it.

This leads us to David's fourth conviction.

UTC 4: DAVID ASSUMED GOD WAS WORKING PROMOTIONS— EVEN THROUGH PERCEIVED DEMOTIONS.

You'll notice that with David, even when things were terrible, he assumed God was working a plan. From the various psalms David wrote, you can see he was convinced that "my God turns my darkness into light" (Ps. 18:28). No matter how dark things were for him, God had a silver lining. So perhaps today, your life isn't as bad as you think. Consider David's twenty-third Psalm:

Even though I walk through the darkest valley, I will fear no evil, for you are with me. . . .You prepare a table before me in the presence of my enemies, You anoint my head with oil; my cup overflows. (Ps. 23:4–5)

To people who believe the Goliath Myth, this is crazy talk, but to a child of God, "surely your goodness and love will follow me all the days of my life" (v. 6). Indeed, goodness and mercy are *stalking* us!

Part of David's optimism was due to his fifth conviction:

UTC 5: DAVID KNEW THAT NO ONE GETS AWAY WITH SIN.

Goliath didn't get away with it, Saul didn't get away with it, and David knew even he couldn't get away with it! David knew that all of us are being tested. All of us are accountable to God. Thus, the last thing he wanted to do was take the risk of committing "reactionary sins" (sins committed out of defense or hurt). He knew God always brings perfect justice—and that's exactly what was about to happen to Shimei.

Eventually, Absalom and his rebellion was crushed, and David made his way back to Jerusalem. As he was about to cross back over the Jordan and repossess his kingdom, guess who fell at David's feet to beg for forgiveness? Good ole Shimei. And once again, Abishai ran to David and said, "Shouldn't Shimei be put to death for this" (2 Sam. 19:21)?

When I first read this, I was thrilled! I started clapping my hands with excitement! I love poetic justice. Here was a man who would have happily killed David if he could have. He had celebrated while one of David's wives was raped in public, and when people are this wicked, they don't usually just "turn it off" unless they're forced to.

If I had been David, I would have said, "Thanks for asking, Abishai. It's time to make Shimei shake!"

Yet, look what David said. "You shall not die [Shimei]" (2 Sam. 19:23). Indeed, the king even promised this *with an oath*. He allowed this wicked guy to live, knowing full well Shimei wasn't the least bit repentant. Shimei was just saving his own skin because he never expected David to return.

Why would David do this? I suppose that, by being gracious, David thought he could stop the blood feud with Saul's family once and for all. Perhaps he was turning the other cheek, hoping the punching would stop for good. But if I can be honest, I *hated* David's response here. As I studied David's story, this passage bugged me for months. The cynical part of me kept thinking that if you don't take out guys like Shimei when you can, they'll come back to bite you over and over. But the real reason I felt this way was because, at the time, I was experiencing a few betrayals of my own.

Over the last two decades of ministry, it's always been painful when people leave our church on bad terms. Like a lot of pastors, my dream is to empower other people to live out their wildest dreams, and unfortunately, it's easy to invest a little too much trust or hope in individuals who simply aren't trustworthy or honest with themselves. The world is filled with people who don't recognize their own motives.

When I was betrayed, it affected other people too. A lot of heartbroken and confused people had to sort through the aftermath. As a pastor I couldn't always share the details—which really killed me in one particular situation. For months people would ask, "What happened with that person?" Many people left our church out of confusion. Others simply accused me of bad leadership, even though their information was extremely limited. Even if I could have spilled the whole truth, I didn't have the time to defend myself. I suppose I could have taken a hundred people out for coffee, explained the truth of the matter; but I would have abandoned my children, marriage, and forward progress to do it. Losing the ability to control your own reputation is one of the most painful crosses of leadership. And, to be honest, I didn't know if I wanted to be a leader anymore.

For the better half a year, my wife and I had to endure endless waves of accusations, misunderstandings, and lost friendships. None of these people knew the information I knew, and they didn't realize that I was feeling the same anger—if not more. As I thought about the people who betrayed me, the same paralyzing questions gnawed at my heart: *What was that person thinking? How did I ever devote so many dreams to them?*

Perhaps you can relate to this experience. I purposefully left out many details because, in some ways, they don't matter. This is the universal story of sin. All of us will eventually encounter someone who betrays us—a friend who makes a thoughtless decision, a lover who rejects, a family member who can't fully see their selfish motives. And in the era of social media, these betrayals can be amplified. Thoughtless people brag up their new lovers, friends, jobs, and churches as if no one in their former world is watching or grieving.

In my particular situation, I knew that generosity was a healthy response, but my question was, "God, why are You taking so long?"—a question David often asked (Ps. 13:2). After all, people are confused! They don't know the whole picture. "*So, God, would you set the record straight?*"

Throughout this time, the Devil often reminded me, "Peter, you have a large platform. And you can use it to defend yourself, reveal people's actions, and change people's futures."

But despite all my feelings of victimization, I remained generous. I focused on ministry. I kept my platform and social media holy. And I trusted that God would defend me and undo the collateral damage. I couldn't shake the question, though: *Have I been a total doormat?* I wondered if my friends and family had unnecessarily suffered because I didn't rise up and deal with the immaturity of the one who had "victimized" us?

So when Shimei seemed to get away with his transgression against David, my heart cried out to God, *Where is David's restitution? How could You allow such a self-centered person to get away with such a low blow?* Shimei triggered a lot of anger in me. Eventually, I shared my feelings with a safe and mature friend.

"Don't you believe in forgiveness?" my friend asked me.

"Well, yes . . . I mean, of course I do," I responded, "but it feels like it undermines justice."

Immediately, my friend pressed me, "Do you really think that forgiveness cancels out God's justice and restitution?"

His question stunned me. I falsely thought that forgiveness meant letting people "off the hook," but that's not exactly the way it works. Even the great theologian of grace, the apostle Paul said, "Don't be deceived: God cannot be mocked. A man reaps what he sows" (Gal. 6:7). Sowing and reaping are some of the fundamental tools God uses to work sin out of our lives.

In raising my children, for example, one of the worst things I can do is to continually protect them from the consequences of their actions, and God is the same way. Sowing and reaping are gifts. Discipline is one of the surest indicators of God's love (Heb.12:6). Some of us would never turn to God unless our escalators broke.

> **FORGIVENESS IS LETTING PEOPLE OFF OF YOUR HOOK AND PUTTING THEM ONTO GOD'S HOOK.**

So as I talked to my friend that day, I realized that forgiveness is letting people off of *your* hook and putting them onto *God's* hook. Forgiveness doesn't negate God's justice. In many ways, it *activates it*. As my friend Nate Banker says, forgiveness is the process of eliminating yourself as the conduit of consequences.

Why would God want this? There are three reasons:

1. God is a smarter agent of justice who is better at avoiding collateral damage.
2. He has greater exploits for us to accomplish.
3. Forgiveness is what frees us up for God's greater exploits. It's a gift that liberates us to live like a child.

So with this in mind, allow me to share one last betrayal story that will forever change how you view God.

THE FATHER OF ALL BETRAYALS

If you paid close attention to the Shimei story, you'll notice that the New Testament betrayal of Christ has a number of eerie similarities (Matt. 26). Christ, a descendent of David, was betrayed by Judas on the outskirts of Jerusalem. And unlike Abishai, the apostle Peter didn't bother to ask his Master about pulling out a sword. He just lopped off an ear of one of the guys sent to arrest Jesus. Yet, after Peter struck the servant of the high priest, Jesus rebuked him:

117

"Put your sword back in its place . . . for all who draw the sword will die by the sword. Do you think I cannot call on my Father, and he will at once put at my disposal more than twelve legions of angels?" (Matt. 26:52–53)

Somehow, in the middle of all this chaos, Jesus had the composure to whip out a miracle and zap the servant's ear back into place!

As I mentioned in chapter 1, a legion could be as many as six thousand warriors, so 72,000 angels is a lot of fighting power! Keep in mind, a single angel put to death more than 185,000 men in the Old Testament (2 Kings 19:35). Jesus basically said to Peter, "Do you realize how much spiritual power we possess as God's children? Do you realize how quickly our Father would defend us if we asked him to?" In other words "Stop flailing around like some powerless victim! Human power doesn't stand a chance against divine power!" Like David, Jesus didn't believe the Goliath Myth. He knew that He could tag his Father in heaven at any moment, and God would jump into the ring.

So in light of these betrayal stories, what can we learn about promotability? What made David so resilient? What caused Jesus to have such incredible composure that, even while being betrayed, He could heal a man? The answers rest in five pillars of promotability.

THE FIVE PILLARS OF PROMOTABILITY

As we walked through the above passages, I pulled out five distinct convictions of David. Now, by observing David's thinking, we can establish five key truths (a.k.a., pillars) that can help us whenever we feel impeded or obstructed by sinful or thoughtless people:

1. OBSESS OVER YOUR OWN CHARACTER ISSUES, NOT OVER THOSE OF OTHERS—focus more on promotability, less on people or promotion.

2. **LET GOD DEFEND YOU**—the more you swing your sword, the more you lose your innocence.

3. **CONSIDER THAT YOU MIGHT BE WRONG**—God opposes the proud but gives grace to the humble.

4. **ASSUME GOD IS WORKING PROMOTIONS, EVEN THROUGH YOUR PERCEIVED DEMOTIONS**—your greatest pains often become your greatest platforms.

5. **REMEMBER, GOD WILL MAKE CERTAIN THAT EVERYONE IS TESTED AND ACCOUNTABLE**—forgiveness doesn't negate God's justice. It activates it.

In many ways, David's is the ultimate story of promotability. He wasn't perfect, but he refused to believe that anger, politics, gossip, or unforgiveness could achieve justice or promotion. And because of this, God said of him, "I have found David son of Jesse, a man after my own heart; he will do everything I want him to do" (Acts 13:22). And as a result, "David served God's purpose in his own generation" (Acts 13:36).

God eventually blessed David with everything: money, mansions, land, and gorgeous wives. Yet God still said, "If all this had been too little, I would have given you even more" (2 Sam. 12:8).

Suddenly, you can see why David is one of the most respected characters in church history. He taught us that no person can stand in the way of your happiness or promotion—except you.

To be clear: God is not looking for *perfect*; He's looking for *promotable*. He already sent His Son to die for our sins. And as you breathe in His Holy Spirit today, He's simply looking for your cooperation (Phil. 2:13). God may not always honor your timelines or agendas, but if you trust Him, He has unimaginable blessings waiting for you—even better than the ones you planned on.

KEY IDEAS

1. It's easy to believe the Goliath Myth, that people can stand in the way of our happiness and promotion.

2. God is so passionate about exposing the Goliath Myth in our lives that He will allow irritating people into our lives until we learn that His power is greater.

3. The moment we think our greatest problem is a person or institution, we reveal that we don't understand God's power.

4. David obsessed over his own character issues, not the issues of his enemies. He believed that, if he took care of his own promotability, God would take care of his promotion.

5. David inconveniently left vengeance to God, knowing that defending himself would only rob him of his connection to God.

6. David regularly considered: *What if I'm wrong?* He gave God the right to use *constructive humiliation* to forge his character.

7. If we do *our* job—which is to stay teachable—God will do *His* job, which is to promote us and justify us at the perfect time, no matter what any man or woman tries to do to us.

8. David assumed, *God is working promotions, even through my perceived demotions.* He had a theology of silver linings even when things were rough.

9. David knew that no one gets away with sin. Forgiveness doesn't negate God's justice. It often *activates it*—which frees us up to become like innocent children again.

10. God isn't looking for *perfect*. He's looking for *promotable*. And the less we focus on people or promotion, the easier it is to focus on the one thing we can change: *ourselves*.

DISCUSSION QUESTIONS

1. David was so sensitive about maintaining his character that he would rather risk his own life than hide even the smallest sin. What might this look like for you?

2. Why do you think it's hard to "allow God to defend us" instead of taking matters into our own hands? How can we avoid "taking up our own swords"?

3. Are you good at apologizing to people? Are you quick to do it? Do you take full ownership, even if you're only partially to blame? If not, why do you think it's hard to do so?

4. Earlier, we defined teachability as "the ability to receive constructive humiliation". Are you capable of handling this from your current boss, teacher, parent, or leader?

5. Does your teachability change from person to person? Should it?

6. How would "believing God is in control" make it easier to be teachable towards others people?

7. Have you ever experienced a demotion or rough spot in your life that ultimately turned out for the good? If so, explain. How might that situation change the way you view your current trial(s)?

8. Why do you think people struggle with unforgiveness?

9. Which one of David's convictions messes with you the most? Why?

10. Which of the five pillars of promotability inspires you the most? Why?

MOTH EATING 101

What Is an External Call and Why Do I Need One?

The first time I ate a moth was on a warm summer night in Wisconsin. Someone left the screen door open, and it was only a matter of time before a baby moth fluttered into our bowl of fresh salsa.

Typical for a group of guys, one of my friends tipped up his chin and challenged, "Is anybody man enough to eat it?"

A moment of adrenalized silence passed. Finally, another friend grunted, "You bunch of pansies. It's just a dead moth!" And with the flare of a pro wrestler, he grabbed a chip, scooped up the moth, and crunched loudly to demonstrate his prowess.

It was like someone flipped a testosterone switch. In seconds, a new definition of manhood had erupted from our salsa bowl. And none were about to be gutless about it.

Every guy in the room scrambled to find moths. As fast as we could stir them into the salsa, we chowed down. Then through the laughter, one guy escalated the standard of manhood: "Come on, guys! Stop eating those wimpy *little* moths. It's time to go *BIG*!"

The stakes skyrocketed. "Oh, yeah? Who needs taco chips? I'll eat a juicy one right off the wall!"

A doomed family of moths trembled on a nearby wall-sconce, but before anyone could make a grab for them, the "manliest" challenge of all was announced: "I dare someone to let a big moth flutter around in your mouth for fifteen seconds and then swallow it down—with no water!"

A holy hush descended on the room. Eyes wide, every man in the room counted the cost. Hadn't we already proven our manhood? Of course we had—but who among us would dare become the *moth slayer?*

"I will!" An older teenaged boy accepted the dare, hoping to sprout a few more hairs on his barren chest. And sure enough, after fifteen seconds of mouth-fluttering horror, he finished the job and sealed his fame forever. That poor moth family never saw it coming, and frankly, neither did I.

As I drove home that night, the effects of the mass hysteria began wearing off. *What the heck were we thinking?*

I was amazed at what a group of friends could persuade each other to do. I doubt any one of us would have tried such a stunt alone. (At least, I hope not!) But that night I learned something about the power of friends: Friends can affect our behavior in some pretty ridiculous ways—for better or for worse. And we're not just talking about peer pressure.

Did you know your friends can actually affect your *physiology*? As I mentioned in *Pharisectomy*, having supportive friends doubles your odds of surviving cancer,[72] stroke,[73] and heart disease.[74] That's right, I said it *doubles* your odds of surviving these diseases. Research indicates that we can significantly predict happiness, stress, memory loss,[75] weight,[76] life expectancy, and the odds of quitting smoking[77] based on a person's quantity and quality of friends! One study found your odds of exercising increases by 37 percent when you have a large number of friends.[78] The implication is clear: God created us to live in fellowship with one another. Even more, your friendships are perhaps the greatest predictor of your happiness.

It might sound strange, but you can actually "catch" emotions like a virus—positive or negative. As I mentioned in chapter 3, people who go to church regularly are 22 percent less likely to be clinically depressed.[79] There's something about hanging out with other people of faith that can actually alter your body's chemical makeup. Even more amazing, research shows that simply "being a Christian" or sporadically attending a church service isn't enough. You have to attend church consistently on a weekly basis and be connected with close Christian friends to experience these clinical benefits.[80]

Conversely, your emotional and chemical makeup can be downgraded when you hang out with the wrong kinds of people.[81] Research on sports teams has revealed that even when a team has an amazing win-loss record the team can have a "depressed outlook" if certain emotionally expressive team-mates are struggling or have terrible attitudes.[82] This is why the Bible constantly tells us to be cautious about our relationships (Prov. 12:26, 13:20; 2 Cor. 6:14; 1 Cor. 15:33; Heb. 10:24–25).

What if your current emotional state is more a product of who you hang out with than the circumstances of your life? Of all the circumstantial things that can affect your happiness, your friends are one of the top predictors—far more than your income, location, or place on the authority chart.

As I've presented this information to various people over the years, the idea really disturbs some of them. Part of this is because changing relationships may require some uncomfortable decisions. It might require you to break up with a boyfriend or girlfriend. It could necessitate switching jobs. It might mean you have to fire a certain talented employee. You might even need to confront a complicated issue with a family member.

Over the years, I've had to make a lot of changes on various leadership teams. Some of these teams were performing well from a numbers standpoint. Yet, their bad attitudes and stress told a different story. In the end, all I had to do was remove a few people and weather the fallout season and, suddenly, everyone was productive and having fun again.

If you're not surrounded by passionate God-seekers who are staying filled with God's Spirit, you'll always struggle to find the motivation and joy that others seem to have. But your relational network can affect far more than this. Your very ability to unearth your calling is at stake—which might be another reason why the escalator towards your dreams feels like it's broken. So now allow me to tell you about a simple concept called your "External Call."

DEVELOPING AN EXTERNAL CALL

Over twenty years ago, I heard a simple idea that has totally changed the way I discern God's calling on my life. I still don't know who originated the idea, but let me explain how it works.

Every calling comes in two forms: an internal calling and an external calling. Your internal call is what you feel you are called to do—e.g., "I think I'm called to be a ballerina, doctor, teacher, or mother." Your external calling, however, is what *other people* feel you are called to do—"I think you would make a great writer, counselor, or coach." You know you're hot on the trail of your calling when they match up. You feel called to be a counselor, and other people feel compelled to pour their hearts out to you.

On the other hand, we've all seen terrifying examples of a mismatch: the 350-pound woman who wants to be a professional ballerina, the

GOD HAS A PERFECT TIME FOR YOU— WHICH MIGHT BE DIFFERENT THAN YOUR TIMELINE— AND GOD IS GOING TO TEST YOU IN THE MEANTIME.

socially awkward pastor, or those people on television singing shows who are convinced they can sing . . . only to embarrass themselves on national television. So how does this happen?

For one, it's clear that many people lack good parenting (or, at the very least, they didn't listen to their parents). Even more, the ultimate problem is the false idea that we only need an internal call to discern God's will. My friend Greg Surratt tells the story of a man who thought he was a great preacher, yet wasn't.

"I have the gift of speaking," he exclaimed with irritation.

To which Greg responded: "You might have the gift of speaking, but do other people have the gift of listening to you?"

It's not enough to have an internal assessment that "you've got the skills." Some people play the "God card," which says something like "God told me to do this!" But this is nothing more than a spiritual-sounding way of being unteachable. After all, God *also* speaks through mentors and authority figures (Heb. 13:17). Thus, healthy Christians are usually capable of allowing godly people the opportunity to scrutinize their ideas.

If you're not capable of handling a decent amount of irritating opinions from people you trust, there's a good chance you'll also be one of those people who is always discontent—someone whose skills never fully pay the bills, a person who's "mad at the world" because you aren't getting the opportunities you think you deserve.

Don't get me wrong. All of us go through frustrating times of waiting and testing. As the Scriptures say about Joseph, "Until the time that [Joseph's] word came to pass, the word of the LORD tested him" (Ps. 105:19, NASB). This means two things: God has a perfect time for you—which might be different than *your* timeline—and God is going to *test* you in the meantime. One of these tests will be the test of your external calling.

Remember, too, that a "calling" literally means people are crying out for you to do it. Yet there are two types of people you can't necessarily trust to give you usable feedback: (1) people who have to live with you and (2) unspecialized encouragers. For example, when your mama calls you "beautiful," it doesn't qualify you to be a supermodel. Or, as another example, married guys know if your wife asks, "Do these jeans make my butt look big?" the only acceptable answer is an instant, "Of course not!" And, ladies, this is a very complicated question to ask your husband for several reasons.

First off, guys love to be experts in everything—even things we know nothing about. If our cars break down, we'll still pop the hood as though we'll discover something new: "Uh . . . yeah. Just as I expected . . . the smoky stuff is coming from the thing-a-ma-bob."

But guys will never be experts in women's jeans because (1) then we'd have to go jean shopping with you—which is worse than being nibbled to death by a bunny rabbit. (2) You'll inevitably ask the "do-they-make-my-butt-look-big question" . . . but on what scale? Compared to normal? Pre-pregnancy? Or are you just talking about "general bigness" compared to the rest of society? (Which, of course, assumes the terrible thought that we've been looking at other women so as to judge.) There's no win here, no objective metrics. So a smart man will always say, "Baby, I am totally underqualified, but you are beautiful to me!" And generally speaking, women will reward this response.

My point is this: When you have to live with people, you choose your battles wisely. Honesty can sometimes fall lower on the priority list—and the same is true when you talk to other people about your external call.

People in my church ask me to mentor them all the time, but what many of them really want is for me to blindly validate all of their preconceived ideas. Unfortunately, I've made a lot of enemies by simply being honest over the years. Therefore, if you really want wisdom from smart people, remember that most will hold onto their best opinion until it's pulled out of them. So be aware of these factors when you seek guidance about an external calling from people who are close to you.

The second group of people you can't trust to validate an external call are the "unspecialized encouragers." At one time, I used to play electric guitar in a band. After one particular performance, a man came up to me and said, "That was some pretty fancy guitar playing." Of course the music we played was anything but difficult, and part of me thought, *Any idiot guitar player could have played what I just played*. But the man was simply trying to encourage me. So don't confuse encouragement with a true external call.

Once you get to know me, for example, you'll find out that I'm a devoted songwriter. I grew up playing almost every instrument. Many of you know from *Pharisectomy* that I used to be a rave/dub-step DJ. (I still spend a lot of time spinning trance music on my turntables.) Almost every night of the week, I relax by writing music in my basement studio—from electronic dance music to orchestral scores. For years, I thought I might be a professional songwriter, but was I good enough?

Over time, I sought the opinions of unbiased professionals. Many of my friends make a considerable amount of money in songwriting, and when I showed them my music, many said, "Dude, you gotta pack up your bags immediately and move either to Los Angeles or Nashville. You could make some serious money doing this." And over time, I continually received this external call from some hefty professionals. On the other hand, I've had other gifts that no matter how hard I tried to advance them, I've gotten a curious lack of interest from other people—like my gift of dancing.

Don't get me wrong. My mom was always there to tell me, "You're so talented—I love you son." But we all need something more than this. Unfortunately, many people never pull out the advice of an objective expert in their field of study. As a result, they stand on a broken escalator that never seems to take them to their dreams.

JOSEPH'S EXTERNAL CALLING

To see a biblical example of this, in Genesis 40 and 41, we read about a person named Joseph. At one point, he was merely a slave who was unjustly imprisoned. Yet, despite his lowly position, he was faithful to use the gifts God had given him.

One day, Joseph realized that he was locked up with the former cupbearer and baker for the king. Each had come to Joseph needing advice on their dreams, and after giving them shocking prophetic interpretations, both of his predictions came true! The cupbearer must have been amazed by this. Shortly after, the cupbearer was restored to his majestic post with the new king. (It didn't turn out so well for the baker.) Eventually, this same cupbearer sang Joseph's praise in front of the pharaoh (Gen.41:12).

The Bible promises that "a gift opens the way and ushers the giver into the presence of the great" (Prov. 18:16), and this is exactly what happened. As a result of Joseph's ministry to the cupbearer, he received the ultimate "external call"—a call to serve Pharaoh himself.

Later, after helping Pharaoh interpret a dream, look at the external call the king pronounced:

So Pharaoh asked [his officials], "Can we find anyone like this man, one in whom is the spirit of God?" Then Pharaoh said to Joseph, "Since God has made all this known to you, there is no one so discerning and wise as you. You shall be in charge of my palace, and all my people are to submit to your orders. Only with respect to the throne will I be greater than you." (Gen. 41:38–40)

So ended one of the most thrilling promotions in biblical history.

In the same way, when we are faithful to serve with our gifts—if we're careful to listen and adjust to the feedback that comes through our external calls—we, too, will eventually use our gifts before "great people." However, if our self-esteems are wrapped around things we aren't meant to be, it doesn't matter how long we wait. We're going to miss the affirmation, the passion (not to mention the compensation) that can only come from our true callings. Life is far too short to wait around for the wrong things, which leads us to myth number eight.

MYTH

THE ISOLATION MYTH:
I can discern God's will and experience healthy promotion without being painfully close to godly friends and successful mentors.

Going back to Joseph, it's important to note that he needed to learn how to wait well. An external call requires patience, faithfulness, and humility, and if you're one of those people who rants that people or organizations won't "acknowledge your talent," you'll repeatedly sabotage yourself.

PATIENCE IS A KEY ATTRIBUTE THAT ENABLES YOU TO SUSTAIN YOUR CALLING, AND IT CAN ONLY BE UNCOVERED THROUGH TESTING.

Leading a church full of young people can get messy at times. Many of them are impatient about their callings, so I'm always reminding them: *Patience isn't the ability to wait, but the ability to wait with a joyful attitude of servanthood.* Patience is a key attribute that enables you to sustain your calling, and it can only be uncovered through testing.

Numerous times over the years, when I was merely days away from offering a person the job and salary of a lifetime, God asked me to test them: *Change his job description or change his place in the flow chart, and see how he responds.* Or, *Temporarily alter her plans and see if she communicates well.* Many of these people had no idea they were being intentionally tested—which is probably good because they would have been totally depressed had they known the opportunity that just slipped through their fingers.

The point is this: Developing an external call requires patience, constructive humiliation, and a trust in the people you're seeking an external call from. In the end, we've got to have successful mentors who can sculpt our external callings. And we've got to have godly friends who can encourage and sharpen us while we wait.

HOW TO BECOME AN "EXPERT"

A while ago, I read about a research psychologist, Anders Ericsson, who made the case that "it takes an average of ten thousand hours of deliberate practice at a skill before you become an expert."[83] By *expert*, we're talking about a person who derives a significant amount of success or income from a specific skill.

When I first read this, it became obvious that true success takes a lot of time! Ericsson's research shows that success takes far longer than we like to admit. When it came to sermon writing, for example, it took me about eleven years to crest the ten thousand hour mark—and that was writing two sermons a week as a full time pastor! How much longer would it have taken had I just written messages once a week or part time? Unfortunately, many people switch fields before they reach their ten thousand hours, which leads us to our ninth myth.

THE OVERNIGHT-SUCCESS MYTH:
Everyone else's promotions come faster than they actually do.

I love to remind people about the full story of Moses. We often forget that when God called Moses at the burning bush (Exod. 3), Moses was already eighty years old! According to Acts 7:23, Moses was forty when he fled from Egypt. This means he spent about forty years in the middle of nowhere—eighty total years before his greatest adventure began.

From an earthly perspective, it might seem that Moses wasted forty years in the desert, but God was giving him all sorts of skills. God knew Moses would be spending a good bit of time leading people around out there so he would need a few desert skills, tent-making skills, and navigation skills. In fact, the route to Midian is strangely similar to the Exodus route.

You see, God doesn't waste anything . . . not our time or our pain. He converts experiences into advantages and pains into platforms. Quite simply, *waiting is not wasting.*

What if your greatest exploits on earth weren't even going to start until you turned eighty? What if everything in your life was simply to prepare you for that? I love this thought because it reminds me that I have a lot to look forward to, and it helps me relax a bit.

Everywhere I go, I meet people who are anxious to "speed up" their promotions. They are so anxious to be married that they'll date all sorts of slimeballs. They take jobs that pull them out of church, or they take steroids to perform better. They acquire unhealthy debt and ignore Sabbath principles to get ahead. But ironically, they're only putting themselves further behind.

I suspect this getting-ahead agenda was on Moses' mind when he killed the Egyptian in Exodus 2. For years, he had known he was going to rescue his people, and he wanted to jumpstart the process. The Bible says Moses was well-educated and wealthy. He had been schooled at the Temple of the Sun—which would be the modern equivalent of a prestigious university. By earthly measures, he was destined for greatness. All he needed was an opportunity to galvanize the Hebrew slaves under his leadership.

And sure enough, one day he saw an Egyptian beating a Hebrew (Exod. 2:11ff). He probably thought, *Perhaps if I fight this Egyptian, everyone will say, "We have a deliverer!"* But instead, his plan backfired. Premature promotions create remarkable demotions. The Egyptian died, the Hebrews rejected Moses as a leader, and the next thing you know, he had lost everything and was running for his life into the middle of nowhere.

Before all of this blew up, though, I'll bet Moses thought, *I'm ready to lead! I'm forty, and I'm not getting any younger! Besides, I've got the ultimate resume!* And on paper, he did have the ultimate resume. What he didn't understand, though, is that God looks at our "spiritual resume"—our character—not our talent or abilities. Like we established earlier, God doesn't look at our *potential* character, only our *present* character. For Moses, God was looking down from heaven thinking, *Wow, Moses! You're not even remotely ready— nor are your people! Arrogant talent is the last thing I need!*

God knew, even after Moses turned eighty, that he was going to struggle with impatience and self-reliance (see Numbers 20). So how much more would Moses have struggled with these issues at age forty? God knew, *If I promote you now you'll end up killing everyone—not just one Egyptian!*

In a similar way, God says to us: "Relax! Stop trying to force everything to happen." Many of us switch jobs, churches, spouses, or cities prematurely (not that you should ever switch a spouse). We compare ourselves to all the wrong people, and our frustrations reveal our idolatries.

THE OVERNIGHT SUCCESS

A while back, I was talking with a depressed church planter who asked me, "Why hasn't the Substance story happened for me? Why haven't we had massive growth at my church?" He was looking at our church and thinking, *What's wrong with me?*

I think all of us have been in that position at some point. We all have dreams that seem slow in coming—financial, professional, ministry, and marital to name a few. So this church planter was looking at me, saying, "You're living my dream!" and he was all weepy and frustrated.

Frankly, I told him, "You're not comparing apples to apples! Believe it or not, your attendance numbers are better than Substance's were in year two! In fact, you're actually doing better than I was. But you're comparing your 'year two' to my 'year eight.'"

"Secondly," my rant continued, "I've got a backstory that you don't even know about! This isn't my first senior pastorate. I devoted close to ten years of my life to another church before Substance—and I couldn't grow that church much to save my life."

"Wow" he responded, "I had no idea!"

"Yeah, there's a reason nobody knows," I explained. "I made all sorts of mistakes! I logged six years as a senior pastor before I even planted Substance. So strictly speaking, my year two at my new church was technically 'year twelve.' I already had about a thousand sermons under my belt before I planted Substance, and you only have a couple hundred!

"Even more," I was cranking up the heat now, "I learned a hundred painful lessons about how to be a good senior pastor before planting this church. And most of those lessons were forged through agony and discouragement!"

Then, I shared all the dumb things I did in Wisconsin. "This was the 'train wreck' that caused me to rethink church governance . . . This was when I learned how to preach differently . . . This was when I learned how to hire, fire, and recruit differently . . . This was the first time I was publically accused of something false . . . This was the first time someone wrongfully threatened to sue me."

After the guy endured my backstory, he finally said, "I always thought Substance was an overnight success, but it turns out, it was over a decade in the making!"

"Forged through pain!" I shouted with drama.

Indeed, most dreams are forged in the fires of mundane faithfulness. Only fools search for success, because true success isn't found. It's forged, in a hot, sweaty room where smoke stings the eyes and soot abounds.

This pastor finally looked me in the eye and said, "Wow! It looks

INDEED, MOST DREAMS ARE FORGED IN THE FIRES OF MUNDANE FAITHFULNESS.

like I'm still building my backstory."

"And someday soon," I assured him, "you, too, will be resented as an overnight success!"

You see, most "overnight successes" are at least ten years in the making, created through unseen pain. All too often, we assume we see what God sees. However, much like Moses fighting with the Egyptian, our premature attempts at promotion only result in exile and death.

The dream God has for you might take longer than you think. So, in light of the time it takes to become a true expert, how can we know if we're spending our ten thousand hours in the right areas?

The way to do it is to surround yourself with godly friends and mentors who can be brutally honest with you. That's what we're going to talk about in the final leg of our escalator journey.

For example, I could practice playing football for ten thousand hours, and I *still* wouldn't make it in the NFL. I simply don't have the body type required to succeed there. Thus, time and mentoring aren't the only ingredients necessary to unwrap your calling. In the next chapter, we'll talk about a final crucial ingredient: the gift of *insight*.

PROCLAIM

Father, help me find the friends and mentors who can help me accomplish the great tasks You have planned. Give me the humility to listen to them. And grant me the patience to do the necessary work. In Jesus' name, amen!

KEY IDEAS

1. Friends can affect your behavior in some pretty ridiculous ways—for better or for worse.

2. Your friends can even affect your physiology, happiness, and odds of depression. You can actually "catch" emotions like a virus.

3. Our emotional states can be more affected by who we hang around than by what is happening to us.

4. Every calling comes in two forms: an *internal* calling (what *you* feel you are called to do) and an *external* calling (what *other people* feel you are called to do). Some people falsely think they need only an internal call.

5. Developing an external call requires patience, constructive humiliation, and painfully honest friends and mentors.

6. If you're one of those people who rants that other people or organizations won't acknowledge your talent, you'll repeatedly sabotage yourself.

7. We're all tempted to believe that everyone else's promotion comes faster than it actually does.

8. Waiting is not wasting. God loves to convert experiences into advantages, pains into platforms.

9. Like Moses, when we take shortcuts to our dreams, it results in unnecessary death.

10. Most overnight successes were at least ten years in the making. Almost all success has a backstory of unseen pain.

DISCUSSION QUESTIONS

1. What's the craziest thing your friends have ever gotten you to do?

2. If friends can affect your life expectancy and happiness so profoundly, what impact might those statistics have on your view of work, dating, church, or family?

3. How might a person "switch friends" in a life-giving way? Can you think of any situations where this could be complicated? Explain.

4. What are some of your "internal callings"—skills, dreams, or vocations that you're curious to explore?

5. What are some practical things you could do to start testing your internal callings?

6. Have you ever met someone with a mismatch (a person who thinks he or she is great at something they're not)? How do you think that person got there? Why do you think they are holding onto the delusion?

7. Have you reached the ten-thousand-hour mark in relationship to any particular skill? If not, what are some of the skills you've been working on? At your current rate, how long would it take before you reach the ten thousand mark?

8. What if God's greatest adventure for you didn't even start until you turned eighty years old? Does that make you sad or relaxed? Why?

9. If God can turn experiences into advantages or pains into platforms, how might this apply in your life? What are some of your painful life experiences? And how could God use them to help others?

10. What is an area of your life where you're struggling with patience? Is there a particular way others could pray for you or encourage you to have extra peace and persistence?

DREAM ACCELERATORS

How Do I Put My Escalator on Fast Forward?

E veryone has a dream. Perhaps yours is to get married, raise amazing kids, or start a thriving ministry at your church. Or perhaps it's to lose weight, get a tattoo across your face, or start a family hip-hop dance crew that puts on shows at local nursing homes. (Admit it, some of you are weirdos.) Not all of your dreams are normal (or even healthy), but hopefully you have mentors who are talking sense into you.

This is why we talked about the Isolation Myth in the last chapter. You need to be painfully close to people who can be brutally honest with you.

"But the senior citizens in my community will love a hip-hop dance family," you argue.

Perhaps so, but what will your teenage daughter think when mom, dad, and grandpa start poppin', lockin', and shockin'? Before you put on matching outfits to share your love for dance, ask yourself: *Do I have anyone who's helping me scrutinize these dreams?* In the end, we don't just want *good* ideas; we want *God* ideas. Uncovering

God's dream for your life requires a bit more thinking, and that's what I hope this chapter will help you do.

Here's a warning, though. I'm going to get super practical. This chapter is filled with soul-searching questions and application steps that may take a while to sort through, but if you pay close attention, this information will be like fertilizer on your dreams.

I'm going to share twelve questions or applications that will accelerate your dreams. I have divided them into four sections of three. The first three is a set of questions to help you discover your calling. The second section includes three tips that will help you accelerate your calling. The third section is a group of questions that will help you discover your mentors, and the final three applications will show you how to get these brilliant people to mentor you.

DISCOVERING YOUR GOD IDEA

Our first set of three is adapted from Jim Collins' business classic, *Good to Great*.[84] Collins argues that "good is the enemy of great." Or as I phrased it earlier: We don't want *good* ideas; we want *God* ideas. Most of us waste far too much time on things we're "good at" instead of things we're "great at." So Collins developed three questions to help companies hone in on their greatest skills.

Although Jim Collins intended for these questions to apply to businesses and organizations, I realized when I first read them that these would be fantastic questions to ask about my personal life too. I've outlined below my adaptations of Collins' questions.

1. AT WHAT ARE YOU GIFTED TO BE THE BEST IN THE WORLD?

Notice, I didn't ask, "What are you good at?" Instead, I asked, "What could you be the *best* at?" When you assess the totality of your strengths, experiences, personality, and genetic makeup, it should point you towards certain tasks. First Peter 4:10 teaches that when we serve people with our truest gifts, it manifests a revelation of God's grace to the world. But this won't happen when we serve outside of our gift mix.

2. WHAT ARE YOU DEEPLY PASSIONATE ABOUT?

What would you be willing to endure huge amounts of pain to accomplish? There are certain areas where you would endure almost anything to excel in them—even boring, tough, or painful tasks. So make a list of them.

For example, you can be extremely gifted at something, but if a vocation is boring or meaningless to you, you'll never stay motivated through the low points. As I mentioned in the previous chapter, I've always received a constant flow of affirmation for my songwriting. Even successful music producers have told me that I should do it professionally. But to be honest, I like pastoring *more*.

You see, it doesn't matter if you're gifted. If you lack the passion, you'll never make it to the ten thousand hours of deliberate practice we talked about. To put it simply: *gifted doesn't mean called*. A long-term calling requires a hard-to-kill passion as well. Even Jesus endured the cross "for the joy set before him" (Heb. 12:2). So, what motivates you like this?

3. WHAT DRIVES YOUR ECONOMIC ENGINE?

Which of your skills pay the most bills? Or to translate Jim Collins' business words into a more personal application: Which gifts create the most resources and opportunities for you and the world?

For example, the apostle Paul was a traveling missionary. Yet, he didn't want to ask people for money, so he designed his calling around tent making. It was an economic engine that opened doors in every city he visited. My question evokes the same thing: What are your tent-making skills? Sometimes, your "unspiritual gifts" can become your greatest tools for evangelism and discipleship— not merely for financial reasons but because success creates respect, which, in turn, can lead to kingdom influence. Many of the greatest disciplers on earth have never been paid by the church.

If you thoroughly answer these questions, it will make a huge difference in helping you prioritize your life. For example, let's say you're equally gifted and passionate about software design and making lifelike ceramic deer statues. Which of these two gifts will result in more money? I could be wrong but probably not deer statues—unless there's a sudden lawn-ornament revolution that will thrust an army of majestic deer into front yards everywhere— which is possible.

"Yeah, but I love making ceramic deer statues!"

"Great," I say, "but make a million dollars on software design *first* and *then* open the world's greatest studio for ceramic deer making. You and your weird friends will have a blast."

Here's the goal. After answering all three of these questions, look at the common denominators. Do any skills, passions, and money-makers overlap? Can you creatively figure out a way to make them overlap? Perhaps Disney World will pay you to design software for a robotic Bambi ride. These questions may take years— even decades—to flesh out. But eventually, you'll find a sweet spot at which all three areas converge. As I like to call it, this is your God idea. If you can devote yourself to this sweet spot for ten thousand hours . . . watch out world! Your gift will "make room for you" (Prov. 18:16), and when you're a billionaire, majestically riding in parades on your robotic deer, you can thank me.

WE ALL TEND TO JUDGE OUR OWN SKILLS BASED ON OUR POTENTIAL GIFTS, NOT OUR ACTUAL GIFTS, WHEREAS OTHER PEOPLE JUDGE US BASED ON FRUITFULNESS, NOT POTENTIAL.

Just keep in mind that you can't unearth your God idea in isolation. In keeping with the concept of the external call, your God idea can only be confirmed by mentors. As painful as it is to listen to outside advice, it's far easier than the pain of self-deception and confusion. Here's why: We all tend to judge our own skills based on our *potential* gifts, not our *actual* gifts, whereas other people judge us based on fruitfulness, not potential. "If I could just sing on *American Idol*." "If the coach would just put me in the game." "If my boss would just give me a shot, then the world could see my potential!" The only problem is that the world may also see you're an immature idiot who has potential but no consistency, or you have consistency with no character, or character with no public-relations skills (or whatever complementary skills are necessary over the long haul). As a result of our individualistic idealism, we become unreasonably irritable with the people who want us to test out our skills or acquire a complementary skill set.

Remember the Talent Myth—the belief that an exceedingly developed talent is the primary ingredient that qualifies you for promotion, more than character, experience, perseverance, loyalty, or leadership? When we imagine our future "dream vocations," we have the tragic tendency to overvalue certain skills to the exclusion of other, complementary skills. This results in a lot of newspaper headlines.

We see this play out with professional athletes every week. Sports stars think their athletic skills should compensate for their bad habit of punching babies while doing drugs. "But I'm an athlete, not a role model!" They foolishly reduce their careers to a narrow set of sports skills, while ignoring all the complementary skills—like good character—that will sustain this primary gift.

Like the immature sports star, we all eventually have opportunities to rant at the coach who's "holding us back." Or we can stop and recognize, "my scorecard may not be the same as those around me." And hopefully, we'll painfully submit to our coach's process.

To put this another way: We all tend to judge our talents with an incomplete scorecard—which is partly why the people around you might be slow to acknowledge your gifts. If people around you aren't acknowledging your greatness, perhaps you aren't listening to their definition of greatness. Or more importantly, you aren't listening to *God's* definition of greatness. Generally, our primary problem doesn't rest with our talent but with our inability to see the greater scorecard.

So how do we discover this elusive scorecard? By painfully listening to Scripture, to godly friends, and to mentors (myth 8). So let's move on to the application steps.

THREE STEPS TO ACCELERATE YOUR CALLING

If you really want to speed up your escalator, pay attention to three practical steps for uncovering your external call.

1. DISCOVER A POTENTIAL GIFT.

Are you artistic, administrative, musical, technical?

2. FIND AN EXPERT.

This would be someone who has already logged at least ten thousand hours in the area you think you're gifted in. And don't find just anyone; find someone who's truly successful and godly.

If you need advice on being a good business person, don't go to someone who's struggling or mediocre. Go to someone who's been defying the odds year after year. Ask that person, "Could this really be my God idea? Do I really have the potential of being great at this if I devote ten thousand hours to it?" After all, you *don't* want to devote ten thousand hours to something you're not really capable of being the *best* at. At this point, your advisor will likely tell you about "complementary skills" that you haven't even begun to think about.

If you discover your calling and an expert confirms it, then . . .

3. LOG YOUR TEN THOUSAND HOURS WITH A TEACHABLE ATTITUDE.

Don't start acting like an expert after seven years. "Yes, but I have a degree!" Great, but that doesn't make you an expert. It just means someone took your money in exchange for exposing you to information. A degree simply means you *might* finally qualify for an entry-level job. But make no mistake, a degree is *not* an external call. In some fields, it's the tool you want *after* you've received an external call.

Here's my main point: *A spirit of entitlement always crowds out a spirit of teachability.* Every dream job requires complementary skills and tasks that are seemingly unnecessary or just plain stupid. Until you're an expert, though, you're not even qualified to discern this. That's what makes mentoring so critical.

Psalm 127:4 says that children are like "arrows in the hands of a warrior." I love this image because it shows how parents and children are supposed to cooperate with one another. Parents help aim their kids. No matter what the age, ideally kids should leave home with a clear sense of purpose and calling. Just as important, kids must remain "aim-able"—which can be uncomfortable. If you endure this process, though, you're certain to go much further than you would have gone on your own. If children and parents have a loving, supportive relationship, God's intent is that we hit targets that would have been impossible for us otherwise.

But what if my parents or former leaders were terrible? you might wonder. Hear me say this: Don't waste even a single second blaming them! God says, "I will repay you for the years the locusts have eaten" (Joel 2:25). If you are an orphaned child, remember, your heavenly Father can adopt you into the greatest of families.

Unfortunately, many of us have been "difficult children." Our unrealistic expectations and arbitrary timelines have often made it difficult for parents and leaders to sculpt us—which could be one of the reasons we were orphaned (just kidding).

Many times, my progress stalled out because I hadn't really been honoring my parents or mentors. As the fifth commandment says, "'Honor your father and mother'—which is the first commandment with a promise—so that it may go well with you and that you may enjoy long life on the earth" (Eph. 6:2–3). Notice, you can honor people (and receive the benefits) regardless of whether or not your leaders are honorable.

"But you don't know how selfish my parents or past leaders were," the whine continues. Perhaps so, but the action of honoring others is God's tool to transform *us*, not *them*. When we honor past and present divine relationships, God creates future divine relationships. Honor isn't something that people merit. It's something that is sown and reaped.

> ## HONOR ISN'T SOMETHING THAT PEOPLE MERIT. IT'S SOMETHING THAT IS SOWN AND REAPED.

Besides, you'll find that your opinions about your parents and mentors will change with time. Once you log a few more humbling years of parenting and leadership, you'll realize your parents and past leaders were probably smarter than you thought. And you'll be glad you didn't burn bridges in your youthful zeal.

God didn't design us to "aim" ourselves. The direction and momentum of our callings comes from the godly warriors around us, and our job is to make it easier for them to propel us onward.

This brings up the question: How do we identify such mentors?

THREE MENTORING QUESTIONS

Every year, I ask myself three questions that usually reveal a few new divine mentors:

1. WHAT IS YOUR DILEMMA OR DREAM?

What problem are you trying to solve? What's the industry you want to be successful in? Or maybe you have a personal problem like, "How do I find a hot date?" Or a ministry dream, "How do I launch this outreach?" Or maybe you wonder, What is God's dream for me this year?

2. WHO HAS SUCCESSFULLY NAVIGATED YOUR DILEMMA OR DREAM?

What person do you know who is living out your dream? For example, if you plan on being married or having kids in the next five years, you better surround yourself with people who have successful marriages and proven parenting skills. They need to be thriving practitioners, not cynical theorists.

3. WHAT ARE YOU DOING TO EARN THE RIGHT TO BE AROUND THESE PEOPLE?

Successful people are usually busy people. The great irony when searching for mentors is that the best mentors are usually people who are too busy to mentor you! Ironically, the pastors or mentors who have "all the time for you" are usually the ones you want to be wary of. Thus your dilemma: *How do you get mentored by people who are too busy to mentor?* The answer is you *earn* it.[85]

One time, I reached out to a well-known pastor and he snubbed me. Well, he didn't actually snub me. As I look back, I was probably ridiculously oversensitive to rejection. I was like a fourth-grade math student who thought I needed a world-class physicist to help with my homework. My expectations were wildly unrealistic. In some ways, I wanted a Yoda-type mentor in my life.

A MENTOR YOU SEEK?

When my son turned six, he became obsessed with pretending to be Yoda from *Star Wars*. He would go for weeks without responding to his real name—which can get really awkward when you're forced to call him Yoda in public. I, of course, became Luke Skywalker, seeking Yoda's advice for everything.

Over time, he began to take this game a bit too seriously. Once when I told him to hurry up and get his pajamas on, he rebuked me in a firm voice: "Padawans do *not* tell Jedi Masters what to do!" And he glared at me.

A bit stunned, I looked Yoda in the eyes and acted out a dramatic spanking motion. "You better get your pajamas on, or I will show you the force on your dark side!" It's amazing how quickly the galactic empire came into balance.

But the reason I bring up Yoda is because that's what I was hoping for out of this famous pastor. I wanted a singular person who could help fill the "father wounds" left by my former leaders or mentors. I wanted him to ride on my back and go camping with me. I wanted to be able to snuggle into his cozy house and hear his timeless wisdom whenever the dark side felt near. My expectations were ridiculous, of course, but I didn't fully learn this until the tables were turned.

Years later, I became the pastor that people would ask to mentor them. They would waste my time left and right. They'd ask for advice but wouldn't apply it, or I would meet with them and they would get offended because I couldn't meet every week. I quickly found out why great leaders create hoops for people. It's not arrogance; it's *stewardship*. If you don't have standards, the Devil will sap your strength through manipulative people.

Several years ago, a young man asked, "Pastor, would you mentor me?" I started asking him questions with the hope of discovering his expectations, and after listening to him, I knew I would disappoint him. I simply wasn't available enough to meet as often as he wanted. So when I turned him down, he walked away dejected. I felt terrible, but I've got hundreds of pastors, interns, and other key leaders who serve twice as much. Even more, I believe God's grace continues to flow when I keep my priorities straight. My capacity increases in proportion to my priorities.

Two weeks later, he came up to me and said, "Pastor, would it be okay if I mowed your lawn for free—all summer?"

"For free?" I asked.

"Yes, for free. No strings attached. I'll just show up whenever and do it."

"Well," I said, "if you really want to, I'm not going to resist it— unless you do a terrible job!"

We shared a quick laugh, and he started coming over the next week.

The third time he worked on my lawn, I noticed he looked thirsty. I invited him in and gave him access to the fridge, and every once in a while during water breaks, he would ask quick questions like, "Hey, Pastor, how would you handle this situation?"

It turned out he had been mentoring all sorts of young guys in our church, and he needed advice. They were never super-long questions, but once I answered them, off he'd go. And he applied my advice right away.

By the end of the summer, that dude had extracted more advice out of me than half my staff had gotten all year. He worked a brilliant plan! Ironically, *I* learned two profound lessons from *him*:

1. If you want to be mentored by someone, start mentoring others; you reap what you sow.
2. Whenever you want to get mentored by someone, figure out a few practical ways to serve the mentor.

The people I need as my mentors are usually extremely busy, so I always ask them, "What can I take off your plate? Is there a person I could mentor for you? Or is there an initiative I could advocate for?" When I serve like this—with no strings attached—I get access to some of the most brilliant pastors in America. Which leads to the final three tips for getting unprecedented access to mentoring.

MENTORING ACCELERATORS

In 2 Kings 5, we read about an amazing leader named Naaman. He had everything going for him—until he contracted leprosy. When the disease took over, he employed a strategy much like the three mentoring questions. He asked: "What's my dilemma?" and "Who has successfully navigated it?" In answer, the name of the prophet Elisha kept coming up, so he packed his bags and made the stressful trip to Samaria. When he arrived, Elisha didn't even come to greet him. Instead, he sent a messenger to tell Naaman, "Go dip seven times in the Jordan River." The instructions didn't make Naaman happy:

> But Naaman went away angry and said, "I thought that [Elisha] would surely come out to me [not his servant] and stand and call on the name of the Lord his God, wave his hand over the spot and cure me of my leprosy. Are not Abana and Pharpar, the rivers of Damascus, better than any of the waters of Israel? Couldn't I wash in them and be cleansed?" So he turned and went off in a rage. (2 Kings 5:11–12)

Fortunately, Naaman had a smart assistant who begged him, "Just do what he says! What have you got to lose?" After relenting, Naaman dipped himself seven times in Israel's river.

I can't imagine how stupid Naaman must have felt while dipping. One, two, three . . . *Why am I doing this idiotic ritual?* . . . Four, five . . . *This doesn't make any sense!* Six, seven . . . but finally, on his seventh dunking, he came out of the water completely healed!

"So what does this story have to do with mentoring and pain?" you might ask. As you'll soon find out, this is the ultimate roadmap for mentoring. It sets up our final three *mentoring accelerators*.

1. SPEND THE MONEY NECESSARY TO MEET ON YOUR MENTOR'S TERMS.

Traveling to Samaria was *not* an easy trip for Naaman. He had to jump through massive political red tape and spend a lot of money. Over the years, I've made many cross-country trips for mentoring, coaching, or consulting. Even now, I have a mentoring budget.

Why? Because if you want good mentors, you need to go where they are and do what they do.

2. HANG OUT WITH THE PEOPLE THEY TELL YOU TO HANG OUT WITH.

Even though Naaman only got to interact with Elisha's assistant instead of Elisha himself, the advice still worked. You don't always need a rocket scientist to make your paper airplane. To *you*, it might be an extremely complicated paper airplane, but throwing a fit like Naaman will guarantee that you won't get help from *anyone*.

One time, a guy insisted on meeting with me instead of my executive, even though I genuinely knew my associate was the better one to help with his issue. But he wouldn't relent. In the end, he totally robbed himself. He got the Loser-Cruiser when he could have gotten the Cadillac. Even worse, his problem needed a follow-up meeting—a meeting I couldn't give him. Sadly, my associate would have been able to accommodate him, but he was too arrogant to receive what God had for him. So remember, your best mentor might be someone's young assistant. Besides, you really need a team of mentors, not just one person.[86]

3. JUMP THROUGH THE HOOPS YOUR MENTORS REQUIRE EVEN IF THE HOOPS DON'T MAKE SENSE TO YOU.

Naaman thought, *Why would I travel all this way to dip in a dirty river?* It didn't make sense to him, but thankfully, he obeyed and reaped the rewards. This is how mentoring works. At some point you have to trust your mentor's direction, even if that person is simply testing you.

Here's a final example of this. For the first decade I was a pastor, I didn't have many spiritual fathers, but a while back I met Pastor

Billy Hornsby and felt like the Lord spoke to my heart: *Get close to him . . . or those who serve him.*

I have to admit that, at the time, I was kind of scared of him. Before pastoring, he had been a Louisiana State Trooper—and he *looked like it.* From a personality standpoint, he was completely different than me. He seemed like an odd fit for a spiritual father, but the Lord seemed to persist: *Do whatever he asks you to do—no matter how inconvenient! And trust him.*

So Pastor Billy asked me to fly places, write curriculum, and mentor other people. Most of this was on my own dime. One time, he asked me to help him write his newest book. At the time, I didn't have enough time to write my *own* book, let alone *his.* There were times when I'd think, *God, did You really want me to do everything he asked? Is this really the best use of my time?*

But I kept on. One time, he asked me to fly to this conservative school in the Midwest to teach a small gathering of pastors. You see, Billy would go to a church, no matter how small. He was never "too big" for an event, but I wasn't that spiritual. My attitude was: "You want me to go *where?*"

Even worse, he told me, "You're gonna have to wear a suit"— which means, "you're guaranteed to hate it." Pastors who still wear suits in America never understand me. I'm a total weirdo to them. They can never grasp why anyone would name their church "Substance" unless they were on drugs. But at the time, Billy was feeling quite sick. He needed someone to tag-team preach with him so he could have a break. As hard as the Midwest trip would be for me, I knew it would be much harder for him. Besides, God had spoken to me, *Do whatever he says!* And as a good son, my job was to say, "*Yes, Sir!*"

I won't lie to you. That trip was tough. Half of the pastors there didn't even want to talk to me. I barely got my own sermon written for the upcoming weekend, and by the end of the event I had almost lost my voice.

But guess what? That was the last time I ever got to travel with Billy. He was sick with cancer, and shortly after that trip he passed away.

At Billy's funeral, I thought back on all the trips I had taken with him, and I realized that almost every good thing in my ministry career came through this one man's life. He grounded me, even as I was swinging theologically towards some silly church methods. He lent me $100,000 to plant my church. And almost every great pastor friend, publishing deal, and speaking gig came as an indirect result of this one man.

Mentors don't always look like you expect, and the hoops you jump through won't always make sense. Promotion never comes, though, without a little testing and pain. And you can't have testing without mentors (myth 8). Your life is the arrow. Your mentors are the warriors.

It's true that an amazing warrior will mess with you—bend you and then straighten your feathers. A mentor will rub you the wrong way. However, tension and testing are not evidence of a bad warrior; they are evidence that you're about to be launched.

The world is strewn with warped arrows, randomly sticking out of the dirt, but you don't have to be one of those. Instead, you can hit the bull's-eye. You can be the arrow that takes down the greatest foes, the Goliaths—and when you do, the world will rejoice with you.

PROCLAIM

Father, give me the grace to endure the divine sculpting You've provided for me. You are the Good Shepherd; I shall not be in want.

KEY IDEAS

1. You don't want "good ideas" for your life. You want God Ideas. When you seek God to discover your truest skills, God adds divine favor.

2. Being gifted in something doesn't mean you're called to it. There are numerous ingredients to your God Idea—especially endurance and fruitfulness.

3. We all tend to judge our own skills based on our *potential* gifts, not our *actual* gifts, but other people judge us based on fruitfulness, not potential.

4. When it comes to our dreams, we all have the tragic tendency to undervalue the skills necessary to fulfill those dreams. We overvalue certain skills to the exclusion of other complementary skills.

5. We often evaluate ourselves with a scorecard that's different than God's (or those around us). Mentoring makes us painfully aware of this disparity—which is better than waiting for public shame to make us aware.

6. We are all like arrows in the hands of a warrior. We weren't made to aim and propel ourselves, and although some of us didn't have godly parents or mentors to do this, God can compensate for that lack in our lives.

7. We don't honor parents or mentors because they are honorable; rather, honoring them is for our benefit. It's a seed that is sown and reaped.

8. The best mentors are usually people who are too busy to mentor you. Any mentor who doesn't set up hoops for you to jump through is probably a bad steward. This is why we need to learn the art of earning insight from great mentors.

9. The best mentors are gained through two actions: (1) mentoring others (you reap what you sow) and (2) serving your mentors.

10. The best mentor for you may be the "young assistant" to the person you want to be mentored by. Don't allow pride and hidden expectations to keep you from divine insight.

DISCUSSION QUESTIONS

1. As you read the first three questions pertaining to your God Idea, what are some of your giftings, passions, and economic engines? What skills, passions, and money-makers are you wrestling with? Do any of them overlap?

2. Have you ever seen someone who's gifted in something but not passionate about it, or passionate but not fruitful? Explain.

3. How long do you think it takes to discover your God Idea? Explain.

4. Earlier, we learned that we all have the tragic tendency to undervalue skills necessary to fulfill our dreams because every dream requires complementary skills to sustain our primary gifts. Have you ever experienced this (in parenting, leadership, at work)? What were some of the complementary skills you had been unaware of?

5. Is there an area of expertise that you've been devoting the ten thousand hours to? If so, as you've logged hours, have you ever adjusted your course or considered changing vocations or focus? Why or why not?

6. Have you ever had a bad boss, coach, or parenting experience? If you were in the same position as that leader, what would you do differently?

7. What do you think "honoring" looks like—for parents, teachers, bosses, etc.? Why do you think God requires this?

8. After reading the mentoring questions (What's your dilemma? Who's navigated it? What are you doing to get around them?), give an example of a current dilemma you're walking through. Which of these three questions is hardest for you to answer?

9. The best mentors are found through two actions: (1) mentoring others and (2) serving your mentors. What are some practical ways you could apply these ideas?

10. Name someone who has had a big influence on your life. Why do you think that person has had such an impact?

THE GREAT WHITE SKIMBOARDER

How Much Pain Are You Willing to Endure?

n Minneapolis, where I live, there are more indoor malls than anywhere in the world. Indoor malls were invented here—and it's no mystery why. When your winters last a while, you need places to go. And since our state has no sales tax on clothing, there are also direct flights from London and Japan for "shopping tourists."

Yet, despite having more than a dozen monstrous malls, Minnesotans felt the need to build the world's *largest* mall, complete with a theme park in the middle. And, then, because that *still* wasn't big enough, we decided to double its size. As you can imagine, it's easy for tourists to exhaust themselves. On a mall tour, they can end up walking five or ten miles without even realizing it. And sometimes the escalators don't help.

I recently came upon a roped-off escalator in a mall department store. The thing was obviously broken, and people milled around the base wondering how to get upstairs. As a young saleswoman approached us, an exasperated shopper squawked, "How do we get to the next level?"

We had already considered the tiny elevator in the corner of the store, but a long line of homicidal moms with strollers were already waiting there, glaring in our direction and daring us to get in their way.

"Is there another way up?" I asked.

In an overly perky voice, the young saleswoman spouted off some directions. "Well, yes. Take two lefts, then walk out into the mall, and turn right. About a block down, you'll see an escalator. Then it's a quick walk back!" She smiled at us as if she had just solved an advanced math problem.

A pool of confused people stared at the sales lady. By the time she finished explaining the long walk a second time, her little audience gasped, as if to say, "How dare you suggest we walk that far!"

I felt an impulse to share a *Braveheart*-like speech with the clerk:

Do you realize who we are, young lady? We are entitled, obese shoppers who won't stand for inconvenience of any sort. Many of us buy ugly "poncho blankets" because we're too lazy to retuck our TV blankets after we refresh our bowl of cheese balls. We've grown up with TV remotes and voice-activated phones. How dare you tell us to breathe harder! Every person shops! But not every person climbs stairs!

Before my majestic speech could begin, however, the group decided: "We don't need to keep shopping here." And we all wandered off like zombies toward the nearby Starbucks. Part of me still wanted to shop in the men's section on the next floor, but another part of me said, *It's just not worth the pain.*

This story pretty much sums up how most people view promotion: I want it, as long as it doesn't require much effort. Unfortunately, though, if you really want to know how to speed up your calling, I can tell you the secret in one word: *pain*. How much pain are you willing to endure?

Obviously, not all pain is good, and it's important that we know the difference between *stupid* pain and *necessary* pain.

THE YELLOW BOARD OF PAIN

A few summers back, my kids bought a slip-and-slide for our backyard. But this was no ordinary yard toy. It was a special skimboarding slip-and-slide, ready for our own backyard X Games. To get your adrenaline pumping, you would run up to the wet plastic and jump onto a yellow wooden skimboard, and if you were really ready for primetime, you could slice across the water for fifteen glorious feet. Because I grew up with a huge half-pipe skate ramp in my backyard, I thought this would be a fun time to show my kids how completely awesome I was.

Now, my beach body isn't as striking as it once was—nor are my extreme sports skills—but like many adults, I'm forever twenty-one. And with my kids watching, I was desperate to prove it. I even told them to keep the video camera running to capture me skimming my way to glory.

Unfortunately, that day my mind wrote a check my body couldn't cash. Instead of skimming to glory, my legs rocketed skyward, and, like a cartoon, my starkly white body hovered for an instant in the air before thundering to the hardened grass below. The oscillating sprinkler sprayed me back to consciousness, but no part of my body was about to move any time soon.

My daughter ran up to get a damage-control report. "Are you okay, Daddy?"

My dazed eyes told her she had reason for concern. I had knocked the wind out of myself. It felt like twenty seconds passed before I took my first huge breath.

One reason I had imagined this turning out differently was that, once upon a time, I competed in freestyle BMX. My collection of hundreds of old fail-videos ceaselessly entertain me, but my new slip-and-slide, backflop video only brings shameful questions like:

- Why is my tan so bad?
- What made me think my kids would respect me more by doing this?
- And why would I record it?

My discernment that day was indefensibly naked.

My wife, who was speaking at a conference on the other side of the U.S., immediately heard about it (through my mother-in-law), which only goes to show that nowadays, your shame can score a touchdown before your game gets off the bench. By the time I got an icepack on my head, my wife had already texted me the time of my newly scheduled chiropractic appointment. In the end, her admin skills were what truly impressed my kids.

In direct contrast to this example of *stupid* pain, there is what we call *necessary* pain. Like lifting weights to get in shape, this is the inescapable pain required to produce results. It's the pain of allowing friends and mentors to critique our previously perfect plans. It's the pain of inconvenient loyalty and faithfulness, and the pain of apologizing, even when you were only 10 percent wrong. It's the pain of being publically criticized and misunderstood. In short, it's the pain of followership—taking up your cross *daily* to follow Christ (Luke 9:23). In a world that's full of myths and shortcuts to happiness, we all have a tendency to categorize *any* pain as stupid pain, but it's not.

In direct contrast to this tendency, I will introduce our tenth and final myth.

MYTH	THE PAIN MYTH: *Promotion should be free of testing and pain.*

The myths in this book are nothing more than the lies we believe in order to avoid necessary pain. They're the shortcuts that short-change us. They're the beliefs that betray us, the yellow skimboards we imagined would glide us into glory, only to leave us flat on our backs—which is how some of you feel right now.

But don't despair! God isn't done with you yet. The only reason I know these myths is because God has used a painful experience in my life to expose each one. As I mentioned in chapter two, people who experience traumatic events report higher life satisfaction than the general population.[87] I'm not suggesting that you punch a wall in order to experience more pleasure, but many of life's greatest joys can only be forged through pain.

THE YEAR MY GOOSE GOT COOKED

A few years back I had a year from hell. Everything that could go wrong *did* go wrong. I lost my ability to talk for the better part of eight months. And when you're a senior pastor of a fast growing church, that's kind of a big problem. To compound the problem, I had to make several deeply difficult decisions about the church and its staff. It was a perfect storm of bad circumstances. And when I tell my pastor friends the full story, most of them shake their heads and say, "Wow!"

In a normal year, I would've pressed into the church like never before. I would've turned on my overdrive. I would've set up hundreds of coffee appointments to smooth over emotions and to keep people happy. But with chronic pain and barely any voice, I had no natural strength to lean on. I was an injured quarterback with no timeline for returning. I even went as far as to wonder, *Am I done with public speaking?* I felt like I had a front row seat to the unraveling of my dreams.

We lost hundreds of members in the confusion. As people grieved the changes, accusation emails and weird personal attacks seemed like a daily occurrence. For the better part of seventeen months, I was totally depressed. I had experienced losses before—but never snowballing losses like the book of Job. Listening to people's opinions in that season felt worse than dying.

In the past, I had experienced three- to six-month depressions and then suddenly snapped out of them. But what do you do when the rain cloud refuses to move? Staying faithful to God in that season was an hourly chore. I finally knew what it meant to "live by faith, not by sight" (2 Cor. 5:7). There were no quick victories or answered prayers to revel in. There were merely seeds of faith, watered with tears. And for some of you, this might be a great description of your life today.

The encouraging news is this: Daylight eventually broke. Depression dissipated. The turnaround took a bit longer than I had expected, but, my fortunes were eventually reversed. My critics were silenced. My reputation emerged even stronger. And the favor of my heavenly Father has been unprecedented.

A few months ago, I was sitting on my back deck journaling my thoughts—tearfully reflecting on many of my losses. Suddenly, the Holy Spirit broke up my pity party with a stunning thought: *All of my most valuable revelations had come from tribulations.* Every current blessing in my life was a direct result of previous

PEACE COMES THROUGH PERFECT SUBMISSION, NOT PERFECT CIRCUMSTANCES.

betrayals. Indeed, my pain was the oven that cooked up this book. My golden goose arrived because my previous goose got cooked.

That's why we can "give thanks in all circumstances" (1 Thess. 5:18), even difficult circumstances, because we know that we serve a God who, in all things, "works for the good of those who love him" (Rom. 8:28).

However, my goal throughout this book has been to prevent you from experiencing *unnecessary pain*. So, before you finish this book, allow me to review of a few of the myths we've uncovered.

THE RECAP OF OUR JOURNEY

We all have a dream of perfect circumstances we hope will make us happy, and some of those dreams were given to us by God. However, they were never intended to be a substitute for Him. Once we accomplished these dreams, we found that the circumstances never fully satisfied us. This is because happiness isn't a circumstance; it's a living being—our heavenly Father. Enjoyment is a gift that comes *exclusively* from Him, and it operates independently of our circumstances (Eccl. 6).

In the end, we don't fully know what truly makes us happy. Throughout our lives, many of us beg God for promotions that would kill us, boats that would drown us, partners who would betray us (myth 3). We simply can't see what God sees. Therefore, we'd all be smart to give Him creative license, knowing that peace comes through perfect submission, not perfect circumstances.

And remember: it will always feel like the people around you get a promotion faster than you do (myth 9). But we rarely know people's backstories. Most overnight successes were actually decades in the making. Many had a broad foundation of godly friends, mentors, or parents who painstakingly paid the price to aim, shoot, and propel that person further (myth 8).

Or, for all we know, that fast-ascending friend has merely graduated to a new level of pain (myth 3). Despite a "move to paradise," that person might be lonelier than ever (myth 4), and regardless, his or her character is certain to be tested (myth 5)!

The lands that "flow with milk and honey" also flow with new temptations and dangers. Great opportunities don't change our character; they magnify and reveal it (myth 6). Throughout our lives, we see thousands of "successful" people crash and burn, but we don't have time to envy or critique them because our own battles are more than enough to occupy us. What we really need is a sturdy connection with the heavenly Father who can deliver us from anxiety (myth 1), free us from our need to control things (myth 2), and convert us back into carefree children. We were designed to dream big, but we weren't designed to control the universe or propel ourselves forward (myth 8). Instead of praying for some elusive opportunity that could change everything in our lives (myth 6), we need to focus on the One who can change everything, the pioneer and perfecter of our faith, Jesus Christ (Heb. 12:2).

Let's stop wasting energy obsessing over people or institutions we perceive to be obstacles (myth 6). Politics, gossip, or anger will never lead us into the peace of God (myth 7). Besides, some of the people you perceive to be getting in your way just might be the very people God is sending to help you (myth 5). Or even more amazing, perhaps God is leading you to help *them*.

In short, pray more for promotability and less for promotion. Work harder to have a heart God can bless and less on doctoring the circumstances that will bless your heart (myths 3, 4, and 5). Let's enjoy the roller coaster of life, like a ride to be enjoyed, more than a trauma to be controlled. And if we do so, we will have a fun road ahead of us—even if we need to carry a few crosses along the way.

As I said before, success is determined by how much pain you are willing to endure. But the good news is that God never calls us to "carry crosses" without a "joy set before us" (Heb. 12:2). Although pain is the ultimate catalyst to promotion (myth 10), our strength comes from "righteousness, peace, and joy in the Holy Spirit" (Rom. 14:17).

So let me leave you with one final exhortation: The Father loves you with more love than you can possibly imagine. He has dreamed of the day you would draw near to Him and experience the fullness of His love for you. He has dreamed of the day you would cast off these myths and begin living a promotable lifestyle. His plan for you isn't merely good. It's mind-blowingly excessive! We will spend forever exploring our eternal vocations together! And it's immeasurably better than anything you could imagine (Eph. 3:18–20).

Our Father "daily bears our burdens" (Ps. 68:19). He becomes distressed when His people get distressed (Isa. 63:9). As you'd imagine, the Devil is quick to suggest that our Father is detached or impersonal, but it simply isn't true. Once you begin experiencing daily deposits of God's love, it will change you into wild dreamers and bold movers. You won't worship sunsets and success, but when you experience them, you'll revel in the One who created them.

After all, here's the final secret: *Most stairways to happiness aren't escalators at all.* They are steep, muddy creek banks begging to be climbed with friends. They are rickety old ladders that ascend into exhilarating dark places. Many people don't even consider climbing them—a lifestyle of myths is good enough for them. But you . . . I hope you will never let these false pursuits be good enough for you.

God has an incredible adventure for you. He created you to worship Him through your taste buds and smiles. He longs to wow you with skies full of stars. But never buy the lie that any of these things can take the place of God and His all-surpassing love. He is everything. We are His, and His escalator is the only way up.

THE TEN MYTHS

1. THE ANXIETY MYTH—

   If I don't worry, my future won't stay on track.

2. THE DRIVER'S-SEAT MYTH—

   Being in control is possible and will cause a lasting feeling of happiness and security.

3. THE OVER-SIMPLIFICATION MYTH—

   Promotion will make my life easier or happier.

4. THE CALIFORNIA MYTH—

   Promotion is a circumstantial or locational problem.

5. THE TALENT MYTH—

   An exceedingly developed talent is the primary ingredient that qualifies me for promotion—more than character, experience, perseverance, loyalty, or leadership.

6. THE POT-OF-GOLD MYTH—

   A golden opportunity, big promotion, or dazzling relationship will improve my character.

7. THE GOLIATH MYTH—

   People can stand in the way of my happiness or God's promotion.

8. THE ISOLATION MYTH—

   I can discern God's will and experience healthy promotion without being painfully close to godly friends and successful mentors.

9. THE OVERNIGHT-SUCCESS MYTH—

   Everyone else's promotions come faster than they actually do.

10. THE PAIN MYTH—

    Promotion should be free of testing and pain.

ENDNOTES

1. Rabbinical scholar Dr. Louis Jacobs argues that the idea of referring to God as Father is a relatively modern notion for Jews. There's been no widespread evidence of this being an acceptable name in ancient or mediaeval Judaism (see *The Jewish Religion*, Oxford University Press, 1995, 164). Some Jews have inferred this name of God from Malachi 2:10 or Deuteronomy 14:1. However, it's an expression unique to the Christian application of Judaism.

2. Messianic prophecies indicated that the "the anointed one" would be born of a virgin. Thus His Fatherhood would naturally be of a divine origin (Isa. 7:14). Or see Genesis 3:15 regarding the unique expression "the seed of a woman" versus that of a man.

3. Fatherlessness increases the risk of violent crime, promiscuity, teen pregnancy, drug and alcohol abuse, homelessness, sexual exploitation, physical health problems, as well as chronic pain issues, asthma, depression, suicide, unemployment, low-income job, divorce, truancy, dropout rates, bullying, prison, and repeat offense. (See "The Vital Importance of Paternal Presence in Children's Lives" in *Psychology Today*, May 23, 2012, Edward Kruk, PhD in Co-Parenting After Divorce, posted at http://www.psychologytoday.com/blog/co-parenting-after-divorce/201205/father-absence-father-deficit-father-hunger).

4. See chapter 1 in Daniel Gilbert, *Stumbling on Happiness* (New York; Vintage Books, 2007), 3–28.

5. Ibid, 5.

6. Daniel Gilbert wrote a fascinating chapter on the prefrontal cortex and its relationship to anxiety. Much of my chapter was inspired by Gilbert's work (see *Stumbling on Happiness*, 11–22).

7. Although numerous studies show this, here are a few of the more robust studies: M. P. Lopez-Larson,; J. Rogowska, P. Bogorodzki, C. E. Bueler, E. C. McGlade, and D. A. Yurgelun-Todd (2012), "Cortico-cerebrellar abnormalities

in adolescents with heavy marijuana use," *Psychiatry Research*, 202, 224–232. M. H. Meier, A. Caspi, A. Ambler, H. Harrington, R. Houts, R. S. Keefe, et al. (2012). "Persistent cannabis users show neurophyschological decline from childhood to midlife," *Proceedings of the National Academy of Sciences of the United States of America*, 109, (2012): E2657–64.

8. M. Meier, et al, "Persistent cannabis users . . ." vol. 109, no. 40.

9. Keep in mind, God doesn't "tempt anyone" (James 1:13), but He will *test* us if He believes we're ready for promotion. And He'll always provide the grace to pass the tests (1 Cor. 10:13). Many Christians have chosen to believe theologies of God that state He creates *both good and evil* (because they unnecessarily conclude that, unless He does so, He cannot truly be "in control"). Although I respect people's interpretations, it's important for people to understand that such theologies undercut God's character in order to resolve logical assumptions about His power. Unfortunately, these approaches to God's sovereignty have always created confusion about the role God plays in difficult situations. Thankfully, the apostle James clarifies that every "good and perfect gift" comes from the "Father of the heavenly light" (James 1:17)—lest someone confuse us about God's character. James clarified a few verses earlier: Evil comes from *us* (James 1:14) not from God. We don't need to worry that our Father changes sides.

10. P. Mensela, et al., "The Role of Adaptation to Disability and Disease in Health State Valuation: A Preliminary Normative Analysis," *Social Science & Medicine* 55 (2002): 2149–58.

11. S. E. Taylor, et al., "Social Support, Support Groups, and the Cancer Patient," *Journal of Consulting and Clinical Psychology* 54 (1986): 608–15.

12. R. G. Tedeshchi and L. G. Calhoun, "Posttraumatic Growth: Conceptual Foundations and Empirical Evidence," *Psychological Inquiry* 15 (2004): 1–18; P. A. Linley and S. Joseph, "Positive Change Following Trauma and Adversity: A Review," *Journal of Traumatic Stress* 17 (2004): 11–21.

13. M. E. P. Seligman, *Helplessness: On Depression, Development, and Death* (San Francisco: W. H. Freeman & Co., 1992).

14. The programming bug (that causes us to think we can control more than we actually do), is probably not a "flaw." According to Scripture, we were, in fact, originally created to control more than we actually do. Thus, perhaps it's a reminder of our former power—a power that was intended to work in conjunction with our Father. When sin entered the world, God decided to leave this part of our brain intact, but it currently causes side effects.

15. E. J. Langer, "The Illusion of Control," *Journal of Personality and Social Psychology* 32 (1975): 311–28.

16. D. S. Dunn and T. D. Wilson, "When the Stakes Are High: A Limit to the Illusion of Control Effect," *Social Cognition* 8 (1991): 305–23.

17. E. Langer and J. Rodin, "The Effect of Choice and Enhanced Personal Responsibility for the Aged: A Field Experiment in an Institutional Setting," *Journal of Personality and Social Psychology* 34: 191–98 (1976); and J. Rodin and E. J. Langer, "Long-Term Effects of a Control-Relevant Intervention with the Institutional Aged," Journal of Personality and Social Psychology 35 (1977): 897–902.

18. The apostle Paul warned us about such people: "Does God give you his Spirit and work miracles among you by the works of the law [quoting all the right Bible verses / making all the right professions] or by your believing what you heard [works vs. grace through faith]?" (Gal. 3:5). Hence Paul says, "Who has bewitched you?" (Gal. 1:5) or more literally, "Who has caused you to turn your Christianity into witchcraft?"

19. D. A. Schkade and D. Kahneman, "Does Living in California Make People Happy? A Focusing Illusion in Judgments of Life Satisfaction," *Psychological Science* 9 (1998): 340–46. However, Gallup's "Happiest States" survey usually finds California in the mediocre or above-average category. So to encourage all my offended California friends: you're special too. However, truly happy people wouldn't get offended. So, in-your-face, California.

20. Ironically, Minnesota, North Dakota, and Hawaii routinely top the list of Gallup's "Happiest States" as it pertains to happiness, emotional well-being, and healthy behaviors. But as a freezing Minnesotan, every February, I still wonder if this study is full of nonsense.

21. Again, in Daniel Gilbert's *Stumbling on Happiness* (which inspired much of this book), he argues that humans have an inability to imagine the emotional details of the future (see pages 102–105 or chapter 5). We have the ability to imagine the facts of our future reality, yet fail to understand how we'll feel in response to those facts.

22. I originally learned this particular idea from John Maxwell.

23. I have no idea which of John Maxwell's books this came from. When searching, I was irrefutably stumped. But it was one of his books from the late 1990's. If you know, tell me!

24. S. Lyubomirsky, "The Limits of Life Circumstances" in *The How of Happiness: A Scientific Approach to Getting the Life You Want* (New York: Penguin Press, 2008), 44–45.

25. S. Lyubomirsky, "Discovering the Real Keys to Happiness" in *The How of Happiness*, 21.

26. If you're interested, I wrote about how I gave my life to Christ in a nightclub in my previous book, *Pharisectomy*.

27. For further reading: the Bible promises that if we find fulfillment, security, and pleasure in *things* more than in *God*, sorrow will increase and grace will decrease (see Ps. 16:4; Jonah 2:8).

28. M. Baetz, L. Balbuena, R. Bowen, *The Canadian Journal of Psychiatry*, April 2013, as quoted by, Graeme Hamilton, "Attendance at Religious Services Lowers Risk of Depression, Study Finds," *National Post*, October 4, 2013. The study followed 12,582 people from 1994 until 2008 who were "not clinically depressed." Researchers made the interesting comment: "[There is] some ingredient of the religious experience other than behaviors, networks or attitudes alone [that] probably contributes to the benefit." i.e. There was some mysterious and perhaps "divine" ingredient that caused people to be happier. Eighty percent of those followed by the study came from Christian denominations. Frequency of attendance decreased frequency of depression even well beyond 22 percent.

29. A recent University of Chicago study known as "the most comprehensive and methodically sound sex survey ever conducted" found dramatically higher rates of orgasms in women who attend church services "religiously." This was echoed by a 1940s Stanford University Study and a 1970s *Red Book Magazine* survey. Both found higher levels of sexual satisfaction "among women who attend religious services religiously." Cited from "Revenge of the Church Lady", USAToday.com.

30. Williams Sims Bainbridge, "The Religious Ecology of Deviance," *American Sociological Review* 54 (1989): 288–95.

31. Richard B. Freeman, "Who Escapes? The Relation of Churchgoing and Other Background Factors to the Socioeconomic Performance of Black Male Youths from Inner-City Tracts." *National Bureau of Economic Research Working Paper No. 1656* (1985), http:www.nber.org/papers/w1656.

32. Chandra Muller and Christopher G. Ellison, "Religious Involvement, Social Capital, and Adolescents' Academic Progress: Evidence from the National Education Longitudinal Study of 1988." *Sociological Forces* 34 (2001): 155–83.

33. Mark D. Regnerus, "Shaping Schooling Success: Religious Socialization and Educational Outcomes in Metropolitan Public Schools," *Journal for the Scientific Study of Religion* 39 (2000): 363–70. Also see Mark D. Regnerus, "Making the Grade: The Influence of Religion Upon the Academic Performance of Youth in Disadvantaged Communities," *University of Pennsylvania, Center for Research on Religion and Urban Civil Society Report* 44/3 (2001): 394–413.

34. Byron R. Johnson, Ralph Brett Tompkins, and Derek Webb, "Objective Hope—Assessing the Effectiveness of Faith-Based Organizations: A Systematic Review of the Literature," Manhattan Institute for Policy Research, Center for Research on Religion and Urban Civil Society (2002).

35. L. H. Powell, L. Shahabit, and C. E. Thoresen, "Religion and Spirituality: Linkages to Physical Health," *American Psychologist* 58 (2003): 36–52, as quoted in the book: *Loneliness: Human Nature and the Need for Social Connection*, by John T. Cacioppo (2009), 261, "Those who go to church more than once a week enjoy even better health than those who attend only once a week. Overall, the reduction in mortality attributable to churchgoing is 25 percent—a huge amount in epidemiological studies."

36. Dr. Robert Hummer argues, "The average religious individual lives seven years longer than the average nonreligious individual, and this increases to fourteen years for African American individuals." Robert A. Hummer, Richard G. Rogers, Charles B. Nam, and Christopher G. Ellison, "Religious Involvement and U.S. Adult Mortality," *Demography* 36 (1999): 273–85. "Research by Johns Hopkins scholars shows that nonreligious individuals have increased risks of dying from cirrhosis of the liver, emphysema, arteriosclerosis, cardiovascular diseases, and suicide." George W. Comstock and Kay B. Patridge, "Church Attendance and Health," *Journal of Religion and Health* 26 (1972): 9–35.

37. For particulars, see L. H. Powell, L. Shahabit, and C. E. Thoresen's study, "Religion and Spirituality" noted above. But many of the studies above also found an exclusive benefit for Judeo-Christian beliefs that went beyond "supportive friendships" and other well-documented protective factors that apply regardless of worldview.

38. How do you find a good church? The top 3 *statistical* predictors of church satisfaction and spiritual growth are: (1) a church where your *whole family* can make a lot of intimate friends (quantity of Christian friends is the top predictor of growth). (2) A church where your whole family can get super involved in ministry. If you and your family don't have a weekly ministry in your local church, your odds of satisfaction and growth plummet. (3) A church where you love the senior pastor. Don't be "called to a church" but not to the pastor. It's like being "called to your kids but not to your spouse." It won't be a healthy long-term environment. Overall, Christians have millions of opinions on church that have a very strong effect on statistical outcomes. I talk a lot about this topic in my book *Pharisectomy*. Look for a pastor you can relate to—someone who's not afraid to wrestle with the inconvenient truths of Scripture yet is simultaneously life-giving (see James 3:17). I personally wouldn't go to any church that allows its traditions to trump its practicality. Nor would I go to a church that doesn't actually believe in and experience present-day miracles. When churches talk about a resurrected Christ with no ongoing resurrection power, it's rather ridiculous. But whatever you do, don't become one of those "independent Christians" who floats, listens to podcasts, and who pretends to do home churches. When we've been hurt by pastors or churches, it's easy to over-react and embrace extreme models of church that aren't conducive to long-term growth. Pretty soon, we have so many opinions on church that we're functionally incompatible with almost every imaginable church. Yes, the bride of Christ (the church) may have a few warts, but the blood of Christ (that

heals us), flows through the body of Christ (His church). A deep connection to an imperfect church might cause a little damage; but a loose connection to church will cause *certain damage* (Heb. 10:24–25).

39. The book of 1 Samuel 2:7–8 boldly states: "The LORD sends poverty and wealth; he humbles and he exalts. He raises the poor from the dust and lifts the needy from the ash heap; he seats them with princes." The book goes on to share story after story of people who've failed to acknowledge this until God's Spirit finds a willing underdog named David sitting in a sheep field. In many ways, all of the chapters that follow are the demonstration of 1 Samuel's thesis.

40. S. S. Iyengar and M. R. Lepper, "When Choice Is Demotivating: Can One Desire Too Much of a Good Thing?" *Journal of Personality and Social Psychology* 79 (2000): 995–1006; and B. Schwartz, "Self Determination: The Tyranny of Freedom," *American Psychologist* 55 (2000): 79–88.

41. O. E. Tykocinski and T. S. Pitmann, "The Consequences of Doing Nothing: Inaction Inertia as Avoidance of Anticipated Counterfactual Regret," *Journal of Personality and Social Psychology* 75 (1998): 607–16 ; and O. E. Tykocinski, T. S. Pittman, and E. E. Tuttle, "Inaction Inertia: Forgoing Future Benefits as a Result of an Initial Failure to Act," *Journal of Personality and Social Psychology* 68 (1995): 793–803.

42. This phenomenon was first popularized by British psychologist Peter Wason— known as "confirmation bias." He proved that we tend to seek out information that already supports our existing convictions.

43. Cited from the National Endowment for Financial Education (a Denver based nonprofit), quoted in the *Daily News* article titled "'I had to adapt to this new life': As Powerball drawing nears, former lottery winners say hitting the jackpot comes at a price," The Associated Press, Wednesday, November 28, 2012.

44. "According to a 2010 study by researchers at Vanderbilt University, the University of Kentucky, and the University of Pittsburgh, the more money you win in the lottery, the more likely you are to end up bankrupt." Quoted in the Yahoo! Financial News article "Riches to rags: Why most lottery winners end up broke," by GoldenGirlFinance.com, Wednesday, 24 April, 2013.

45. "According to Bloomberg's study, state-run lotteries 'have the worst odds of any form of legal gambling' in America. They're so bad that when you play the lottery in Louisiana, over time you're going to average $0.51 in 'winnings' for every dollar you pay to play. The best odds in the nation can be found in Massachusetts, but even up there you're looking at a $0.72 payback on each $1 lottery ticket. And the average payout is just $0.60." Cited by Rich Smith's article, "Who Are the Nation's Biggest Suckers? Lottery Players," at DailyFinance. com; March 27, 2012.

46. Dr. Douglass Weiss, PhD, *Clean: A Proven Plan for Men Committed to Sexual Integrity* (Nashville: Thomas Nelson, 2013), 73. This is a fantastic book filled with a healthy mix of science and proven counseling methods.

47. Ibid., 70.

48. Ibid., 71.

49. It's interesting to note that, even today, this is true. There are over twenty-five major university studies showing that when kids are raised in homes "without their biological mother and father in a low conflict marriage" the odds of healthy child-outcomes plummets. Thus, it shouldn't surprise us to discover that in every state and country where marriage laws have been changed to accommodate sexual preferences and simplify divorce, child-outcomes have generally plummeted. Sure, there may be ways to mitigate this correlation; but, much like second-hand smoking laws, sometimes the freedoms of adults need to be surrendered to the needs of children.

50. James M. Freeman, "Molech," *Manners and Customs of the Bible* (New Kensington, PA; Whitaker House, 1996), 93.

51. China, South Korea, Japan, and the U.S. alone spend $86.4 billion/year. Imagine if we added Western Europe, Eastern Europe, Soviet Union, and Africa. As quoted from Weiss, *Clean*, 7.

52. See "State of the World's Children," 2010 pdf-formatted document, UNICEF, 18–19.

53. See A. Bridges and R. Wosnitzer (2007). "Aggression and sexual behavior in

bestselling pornography: A content analysis update." *International Communication Association.*

54. As reported by Mike Embley, BBC World News, interviewing Susan Bissell, Global Head of UNICEF, September 4, 2014.

55. As reported by the National Center for Missing and Exploited Children, 2013, close to half of all trafficked women are forced to do pornography; see, http://humantraffickingsearch.net/wp/the-connection-between-sex-trafficking-and-pornography/

56. The Hebrew word for circumcision, *mool*, means "to cut away." Keep in mind, circumcision had already been practiced for a while. God required all of the descendants of Abraham to do this as a symbol of the covenant (Gen. 17:10). Abraham may have interpreted this ritual to reveal that only God gives life. The generation coming out of Egypt had already circumcised themselves, but the generation born in the wilderness had not yet experienced this. Certainly, the Abrahamic covenant would have been taught at this moment. After seeing God miraculously part the Jordan River this ritual was probably a lot easier to embrace than I humorously imply. In contrast to the Canaanites, this ritual would have taken on more meaning—such as a radical commitment to sexual purity.

57. Kevin Dutton, *The Wisdom of Psychopaths: What Saints, Spies, and Serial Killers Can Teach Us About Success* (New York: Scientific American 2012), 162.

58. Once again, according to Kevin Dutton's nationwide survey, law enforcement ranks as the seventh most likely profession—after CEO's which were (1), lawyers (2), media personalities (3), salespeople (4), surgeons (5), and journalists (6).

59. Remember, forgiveness is a process, not a moment. And *effective* forgiveness can't be achieved until we realize (1) how deeply we hurt God through our own sin; (2) how profound God's mercy was when He sent His Son to die for us; (3) that usually when we're hurt, there's more than one person to forgive (e.g., the person who hurt you and the people who enabled him or her to hurt you); thus, effective forgiveness requires us to evaluate a lot of relationships and forgive *multiple* people; (4) that effective forgiveness requires boundary-making—a new set of rules to prevent subsequent hurts. Without new and accountable boundaries, there won't be a sense of safety. Healing can't occur without a newly estab-

lished sterile or safe atmosphere. (5) Effective forgiveness requires a full confidence that justice will be served—if not by man, then by God. And ultimately,
(6) it requires restitution for our loss. Sometimes, it can take a while before God
works things out to our benefit. But when any of these steps are hindered, our
ineffective forgiveness will inevitably sabotage some other area. As the Francis-
can friar, Richard Rohr once wrote: "Pain that is not transformed is transmitted."

60. As another example of this, see Jonathan and his armor bearer in 1 Samuel
14:6ff. While Saul and his 600 weaponless soldiers sulked under a tree, Jonathan and his armor bearer decided "Nothing can hinder the LORD from saving,
whether by many or by few." The author of 1 Samuel is trying to illustrate that
godly leaders shouldn't glorify the system that's oppressing them by obsessing
over it. Rather, they "set an example for the believers in speech, in conduct, in
love, in faith and in purity" (1 Tim. 4:12). And please don't misunderstand me to
be minimizing the reality or pain of discrimination. We absolutely need to fight
all forms of systematic oppression on planet earth and fight for racial reconcilia-
tion. However, I'm simply showing how to remain life-giving and avoid a victim
mentality while responding to oppression.

61. The mere process of "adopting a social identity associated with perceived
discrimination" is known to "make a person more vulnerable to depression"
according to a 2010 study of First Nations adults in Canada by research psychologist Amy Bombay, Carleton University. The study was quoted in the article
"The New Group Therapy," *Scientific American Mind*, September/October 2014,
63, by Tegan Cruwys, S. Alexander Haslam, Genevieve A. Dingle.

62. Psalm 56:8 says that God even "records" our tears.

63. Referenced by Joel Stein's *Time* magazine article, "Millennials: The Me Me
Me Generation."

64. "Why Is Narcissism Increasing Among Young Americans?: Play deprivation
may underlie the increase in narcissism and decline in empathy," *Psychology
Today*, published on January 16, 2014 by Peter Gray in *Free to Learn* (New
York: Basic Books, 2015).

65. Here are two self-tests that can accurately predict your likelihood of over-re-
acting to delays, criticism, and coaching: (1) The NPI, developed by Raskin and

Hall (1979), is based on the actual DSM-III definition of the disorder. Keep in mind that you have to be brutally honest for it to work. Also remember that even if you scored high, it doesn't mean you have an official disorder, but it will predict future conflict if you're not aware. The online test is found here: http:// personality-testing.info/tests/NPI.php (2) The Interpersonal Reactivity Index measures your empathy (i.e., your likelihood of putting yourself in another person's shoes). Linked here: http://fetzer.org/sites/default/files/images/stories/pdf/ selfmeasures/EMPATHY-InterpersonalReactivityIndex.pdf

66. Sadly, 91 percent of Millennials expect to stay in a job for less than three years, which could have a devastating effect on their careers. See Jeanne Meister, "Job Hopping Is the 'New Normal' for Millennials: Three Ways to Prevent a Human Resource Nightmare," posted at www.forbes.com, August 14, 2012.

67. This is especially true in pastoral ministry jobs. I've noticed that pastors tend to double their influence and impact every year they stay at a church—assuming they're healthy and good at what they do. So I generally won't hire or promote people if I don't think they'll be around for at least six to ten years. Otherwise, it has a traumatic affect on the emotional and financial health of the church community. Of course, God always has the veto.

68. Consider Starbuck's Coffee: after experiencing constant turnover with their employees, the company realized it cost far too much to keep training new employees. So, Starbucks started to reward faithfulness and loyalty by paying college tuition for any employee making a four-year commitment.

69. For Example: 1 Samuel 2:9 "[The LORD] will guard the feet of his faithful servants, but the wicked will be silenced in the place of darkness. It is not by strength [or, talent] that one prevails." (Also 1 Sam. 26:23 and Matt. 25:21.)

70. We actually get to see David's repentance in Psalm 51, which scholars believe occurred right after his sin with Bathsheba was discovered: "Create in me a pure heart, O God, and renew a steadfast spirit within me" (v. 10).

71. Matt Keller brilliantly expands on this idea in his upcoming book, *The Key to Everything* (Thomas Nelson) releasing in late 2015.

72. F. A. Colon, A. L. Callies, M. K. Popkin, and P. B. McGlave, *Psychosomatics*

32 (1991): 420–25. For further examples, see Will Miller, PhD and Glen Sparks, Refrigerator Rights (Anderson, IN; White River Press, 2007), 137–143.

73. Jolanda Jetten, Catherine Haslam, S. Alexander Haslam, and Nyla R. Branscombe, "The Social Cure,"*Scientific American Mind*, 28.

74. J. Lynch, *The Broken Heart: The Medical Consequences of Loneliness* (New York: Basic Books, 1977), 239–242. See also A. J. Icposowa "Marital Status and Suicide in the National Longitudinal Mortality Study," *Journal of Epidemiology and Community Health* (2000), 54, 254261

75. Jetten, et al, "The Social Cure," 28.

76. Jonah Lehrer, "The Buddy System: How the Medical Data Revealed Secret to Health and Happiness," *Wired Magazine*, 17/10 (2009): 1.

77. Ibid.

78. L. C. Hawkly and J. T. Cacioppo, "Aging and Loneliness: Downhill Quickly?" *Current Directions in Psychological Science* 16 (2007): 187–91.

79. M. Baetz, et al.

80. As one example of many, in the book *The How of Happiness*, Sonja Lyubomirsky talked about a study on volunteerism. Researchers studied a large group of people who had an unpaid role in which they "helped others." And then, after comparing this group to a large group of people who didn't volunteer anywhere, they wanted to find out if there were any disparities in lifestyle satisfaction. They found that, "those who volunteered experienced seven times more life satisfaction than those who didn't volunteer." Even stranger, when the acts of kindness happened on a single day, (say for example, a Sunday), people experienced a "significant elevation in their happiness." (127).

81. The mere process of "adopting a social identity associated with perceived discrimination" is known to "make a person more vulnerable to depression" according to a 2010 study of First Nations adults in Canada by research psychologist Amy Bombay, Carleton University. Study was quoted in Tegan Cruwys, S. Alexander Haslam, Genevieve A. Dingle, "The New Group Therapy," *Scien-*

tific American Mind, September/October 2014, 63.

82. See Daniel Goleman, *Primal Leadership: Unleashing the Power of Emotional Intelligence.* Goleman explains how emotions actually can spread like a virus. (Boston: Harvard Business School Publishing, 2002), 7, 10.

83. K. Anders Ericsson, ed. *The Cambridge Handbook of Expertise and Expert Performance* (Cambridge: Cambridge University Press, 2006).

84. Jim Collins, *Good to Great: Why Some Companies Make the Leap. . . and Others Don't* (New York: Harper Business, 2001).

85. Some people dislike the third question, *What are you doing to earn the right to get around these people?* Weak disciples act like they're entitled to mentoring, as if a good discipler should never demand benchmarks. However, Jesus regularly set up requirements for discipleship (see Luke 9:23; 57–62; 14:27), and He turned people away. He regularly required His disciples to do strange things (see Matt. 17:27; 21:2–3; Luke 5:4–5). Why? Because obedience and teachability matter. Jesus' time mattered. Christ-like discipleship will always cost us something, but that cost is always worth it.

86. No single person is smart enough to give you all the insight you need. You need a team of mentors, and the team will have varying degrees of intimacy with you. For example, I've got inspirational role models who mentor me through their books, messages, and conferences. Then I have coaches: people who are older, wiser, and are willing to hang from time to time. Then I have peers: people in a similar season of life who have fun troubleshooting their problems alongside me. And then I have consultants: wise people I can pay for advice. Inspirational role models probably won't have the time. I often go to their associates and ask them to recommend a few people I could seek out. From this, I assemble a team of mentors, assuming these people have "divine chemistry" with me.

87. P. Mensela et al., "The Role of Adaptation to Disability and Disease in Health State Valuation: A Preliminary Normative Analysis," *Social Science & Medicine* 55 (2002): 2149–58.

ABOUT THE AUTHOR

While working in a nightclub as a rave-DJ, Peter challenged the God of the universe to "reveal Himself" in an unmistakable way. Only seconds later, God responded with a jaw-dropping gospel encounter that shook the foundation of Peter's life. Since converting to Christianity on the spot, he has travelled the world, sharing his radical story and calling others to experience the same joy and power.

Within a few short years, Peter was sucked into full-time ministry. After pastoring in Wisconsin for a decade, Peter relocated to Minneapolis, Minnesota, in 2004 to plant an arts-oriented multisite church called Substance. Within a few short years, Substance became one of the fastest growing and most youthful mega-churches in the United States. Over 70 percent of the thousands who participate in the church community are under thirty years old and over 41 percent of the congregation did not attend church or have a relationship with God even two years ago.

Both Peter and his church are known for their appeal to artists, intellectuals, and unchurched twentysomethings. Not surprisingly, their innovative approaches to worship, film, and church methodology have garnered international attention. Peter also consults with church planters and pastors all over the globe as he serves on the lead team of the Association of Related Churches (www.arcchurches.com).

With a unique blend of comedian, futurist, nerdy researcher, and Bible teacher, Peter released his first national book in 2012, *Pharisectomy: How to Remove Your Inner Pharisee and Other Religiously Transmitted Diseases*. The strange mixture of comedy and spiritual growth launched *Pharisectomy* to become a bestseller on amazon.com. (See www.myhealthychurch.com for more resources and details.)

Beyond family and church, his next greatest passions are music, film, and comedy. Playing just about every instrument from cello to electric guitar, Peter spends most of his free time in his recording studio writing everything from electronic dance music to classical film soundtracks. And he still spins his turntables on many weekends!

Peter currently resides in Minneapolis with his wife, Carolyn, and their three kids. Visit peterhaas.org or Substancechurch.com to download books, sermons, and other free resources. You may also follow him on twitter and instagram at: *peterhaas1*.

FOR MORE INFORMATION

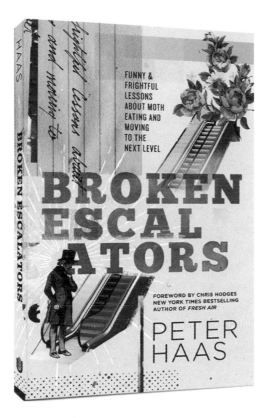

For more information about this book and other valuable resources visit www.salubrisresources.com